NORTHWEST *Fresh* COOKBOOK

A CELEBRATION OF NORTHWEST COOKING AND LIFESTYLE

The purpose of the Junior League of Yakima, Washington (J.L.Y., Inc.) is exclusively educational and charitable and is to promote voluntarism, to develop the potential of its members for voluntary participation in community affairs and to demonstrate the effectiveness of trained volunteers.

All publication sales of NORTHWEST FRESH will be used to support the purpose and programs of the J.L.Y., Inc.

First Printing: September 1, 1990; 10,000 copies.

To order additional copies of NORTHWEST FRESH, please use the forms provided in the back of the book or write to:
NORTHWEST FRESH
5000 West Lincoln Avenue
Yakima, Washington 98908

Library of Congress Catalog Card Number
ISBN # (Pending)

Printed in the United States of America
Shields Printing
1010 Rock Avenue
Yakima, Washington 98902

TABLE OF CONTENTS

APPETIZERS AND BEVERAGES

APPETIZERS AND BEVERAGES

SOY SESAME ASPARAGUS

This looks sensational in an oriental style serving dish.

3 teaspoons sugar
3 teaspoons sesame oil
6 teaspoons soy sauce
1-pound asparagus spears, trimmed and blanched
1 tablespoon roasted sesame seeds

Blend the sugar, sesame oil and soy sauce. Marinate the blanched asparagus for at least four hours in the refrigerator. To serve, arrange asparagus in low, flat dish with spears all pointing in the same direction. Pour marinade over all, and sprinkle with sesame seeds.

FRIED BABY ARTICHOKES

Baby artichokes are so tender the choke can be eaten.

12 baby artichokes, 2 to 3-inches long
2 eggs, beaten
¾ cup fine dry bread crumbs
2 tablespoons Parmesan cheese, grated
¼ teaspoon salt
⅛ teaspoon black pepper
¼ teaspoon oregano
Oil for deep frying

Serves 4 to 6.

Cook whole artichokes in ½-inch boiling, salted water for 20 to 30 minutes or until tender. Test underside of artichokes for tenderness with fork. Drain well. Dip artichokes in beaten eggs, then roll in mixture of bread crumbs, Parmesan cheese, salt, pepper and oregano. Fry until golden brown in oil heated to 360°.

SMOKED SALMON MOUSSE

A fish-shaped mold will create a beautifully eye-catching mousse for that special cocktail party.

⅓-pound smoked salmon
2 green onions, chopped
9-ounces cream cheese, softened
3 tablespoons butter, softened
2 tablespoons sour cream
3 tablespoons lemon juice
Tabasco sauce
Lettuce leaves
Crackers or thin-sliced French bread

Makes 2½ cups.

In the bowl of a food processor, combine the salmon and green onion. Blend well.

With the processor running, gradually add the cream cheese, butter, sour cream, lemon juice and Tabasco to taste and blend until smooth.

Line a quart mold with plastic wrap, pack the mousse into the mold and chill until set.

To serve, unmold the mousse onto a serving platter lined with lettuce leaves and surround it with crackers or thinly sliced French bread.

SMOKED SALMON CORNUCOPIAS

3-ounces cream cheese, room temperature
2 to 3 teaspoons horseradish
1 tablespoon snipped fresh chives
¼-pound thinly sliced smoked salmon

Serves 8.

Blend cream cheese, horseradish and chives in small bowl. Divide mixture among salmon slices and spread evenly. Form each slice into cornucopia. Arrange on platter and serve.

CHEESE TORTA WITH SMOKED SALMON

A very impressive appetizer.

1-pound unsalted butter
1-pound cream cheese
1 lemon
½-pound smoked salmon
Parsley
Cheesecloth

Serves 12.

Line a one-quart mold with cheesecloth which has been dampened and wrung out. Cut butter into cubes and mix with cream cheese until smooth, using steel knife. Slice lemon and put three slices in bottom of mold. Place about 1/5 of the butter mixture in mold, spreading smoothly. Bone and flake salmon. Add half the salmon to the mold, then continue layering with butter and salmon, topping with butter. Refrigerate one hour, then remove from mold and pull cheesecloth off gently. (If left longer the cheesecloth will cause color to spread to butter.) Place on a platter and garnish with parsley and lemon. Serve with a bland cracker or French bread. Also try with Gorgonzola cheese, pesto or sundried tomatoes in place of salmon.

BAY SCALLOPS WITH LIME AND MINT

1-pound bay scallops
1½ teaspoons salt
¼ cup plus 1 tablespoon lime juice
1 teaspoon grated lime zest
½ cup red onion, finely chopped
1 clove garlic, minced
Freshly ground black pepper
¼ teaspoon cayenne
½ cup vegetable oil
¼ cup fresh mint, chopped
2 ripe avocados
½ lime, to rub on avocado
Mint garnish

Makes 4 or 6 servings as an appetizer.

Wash scallops with cold water and dry. Toss in a bowl with ½ teaspoon salt, ¼ cup lime juice and lime zest, cover and refrigerate. Let the scallops marinate for at least 6 hours, stirring occasionally. When they are fully "cooked" they will be firm and opaque white.

Soak the chopped red onion in cold water for 20 minutes. Squeeze gently, dry, and set aside.

Just before serving, make the dressing by combining the remaining teaspoon salt and tablespoon lime juice with garlic, several grinds of black pepper and cayenne in a large bowl. Slowly whisk in vegetable oil.

Drain scallops and toss them with the dressing, red onions and mint. Adjust the seasoning and serve immediately on avocado halves that have been pitted and rubbed with lime. If serving as an appetizer peel and slice the avocados and drizzle some dressing over them. Lay slices on individual serving plates in a decorative fashion and mound the scallops on top. Garnish with fresh mint.

SHRIMP SAGANAKI

8-ounces artichoke hearts, water packed or frozen
4 tablespoons olive oil
1-pound cooked shrimp, medium size
¼-pound small whole mushrooms
2 cloves garlic, finely minced
½ teaspoon salt
Freshly ground pepper, to taste
½ teaspoon dried oregano, crumbled
2 tablespoons lemon juice
2 tablespoons parsley, finely chopped

Makes 3 dozen appetizers.

Drain artichoke hearts. If artichokes are frozen, blanch in boiling salted water for 2 minutes; drain. Heat olive oil in a frying pan; add shrimp and mushrooms and cook, stirring. Add artichoke hearts, garlic, salt, pepper and oregano; heat until hot through. Sprinkle with lemon juice and stir lightly to blend flavors; sprinkle with parsley. Place over a warmer to keep hot.

Serve with toothpicks.

GARLIC PRAWNS

A real show stopper. Be prepared to make more.

4 cloves garlic
½ teaspoon salt
2 teaspoons peppercorns, coarsely crushed
2 teaspoons lemon juice
1 tablespoon brandy
1-pound fresh prawns, shelled, cleaned, split lengthwise
Olive oil
Parsley

Serves 6 to 8.

In a small bowl, crush garlic with salt. Add pepper, lemon juice and brandy. Mix well.

Place prawns in large, heavy skillet over medium heat. Add garlic mixture and enough olive oil to just cover. Saute prawns quickly just until color changes.

Serve hot, garnished with parsley.

SHRIMP DIP

2 tablespoons butter
2½ tablespoons flour
½ cup cold water
1 cup sugar
1 cup onion, chopped
12 tablespoons vinegar
4 tablespoons Worcestershire sauce
Dash soy sauce
Dash garlic salt
Dash pepper
2 cups ketchup
3 6½-ounce cans shrimp

Serves 8 to 10.

Combine butter, flour and water in large saucepan over medium heat. Stir until pasty. Add sugar and onion. Keep stirring and add all remaining ingredients except shrimp. Cook for 15 minutes or until onion is clear. Then add shrimp and continue cooking for 10 minutes. Serve hot with chips or crackers.

CASHEW SESAME CHICKEN

May also be served as a main dish over rice.

Marinade:
1 small clove garlic, peeled
1-inch square ginger, chopped
1 large egg
2 tablespoons dry sherry
1 tablespoon lemon juice
1 tablespoon lemon rind
1 teaspoon soy sauce
¼ teaspoon salt

1-pound boneless chicken breast,
cut into 1-inch pieces

Chicken Coating:
1 cup unsalted dry roasted cashews
½ cup sesame seeds
¼ cup cornstarch

Dipping Sauce:
1 12-ounce jar apricot jam
1 teaspoon dry mustard
1 teaspoon lemon rind
1 teaspoon orange rind
Vegetable oil for deep frying

Serves 12.

Drop garlic and ginger thru food processor feed tube with metal blade and chop for 10 seconds. Add remaining ingredients for marinade and pulse about 4 times.

Place 1 plastic food storage bag inside another and put chicken inside. Pour in marinade. Seal each bag and turn to coat chicken. Place in large bowl and marinate at room temperature for 3 hours, or in refrigerator overnight.

Chop cashews finely, 10 seconds, and mix with sesame seeds. Place chicken coating in bowl and stir in cornstarch. Heat 2-inches oil to 375°. Roll chicken in nut mixture and fry in batches until golden brown or about 3 minutes.

To make dipping sauce, process all ingredients until combined.

CABBAGE AND APPLE EN CROUTE

2 tablespoons butter
1 tablespoon sugar
1½ teaspoons lemon juice
3 cups shredded green cabbage
½ cup shredded tart apple
¼ cup chopped onion
¼ teaspoon salt
¼ cup dairy sour cream
5 frozen phyllo pastry sheets, thawed
⅓ cup butter, melted
¼ cup dry bread crumbs

Serves 6 to 8.

In large skillet, melt 2 tablespoons butter. Add sugar and lemon juice; stir until sugar dissolves. Add cabbage, apple, onion and salt. Cook over medium-high heat 7 to 10 minutes or until vegetables are tender, stirring occasionally. Drain. Add sour cream; mix well.

Heat oven to 350°. Lightly grease cookie sheet. Place 1 phyllo sheet on prepared cookie sheet. Brush with melted butter; sprinkle with about 2 teaspoons bread crumbs. Continue layering the remaining 4 sheets phyllo dough, brushing each with butter and sprinkling with crumbs. Place cabbage mixture in 2-inch wide strip 4-inches from short side of phyllo sheets and 1½-inches from long sides of phyllo sheets. Fold 1½-inch sides over cabbage. Fold 4-inch side over cabbage mixture; continue to roll up jelly-roll fashion. Place cabbage roll seam side down; brush with remaining melted butter. Bake at 350° for 30 to 35 minutes or until golden brown and crisp. Allow to stand 5 minutes before slicing.

MUSHROOM CURLS

These are so easy to make ahead and have waiting in the freezer just to be brushed with butter and baked.

1-pound mushrooms, finely chopped
½ cup butter
6 tablespoons flour
1½ teaspoons salt
2 cups cream
2 teaspoons lemon juice
1 teaspoon onion salt
2 loaves sliced white sandwich bread
4 tablespoons butter, melted

Makes 7 to 8 dozen.

Sauté the mushrooms in the butter for 5 minutes. Remove from heat and cool slightly. Add the flour and blend well, then add the salt. Stir in the cream and cook, stirring constantly, until thick. Add the lemon juice and onion salt, and cool. Remove the crusts from the bread and roll slices very thin with a rolling pin. Spread 2 tablespoons mushroom mixture on each slice of bread and roll up. Place seam side down on a baking sheet lined with waxed paper. Place in the freezer for at least 1 hour. Cut rolls into thirds, brush with melted butter, and bake for 15 to 20 minutes at 400°.

HERBAL CHEESE SPREAD

2 8-ounce packages cream cheese, softened
1 cup unsalted butter, softened
⅓ cup heavy or whipping cream
1 tablespoon fresh lemon juice
1 tablespoon fresh chives, minced
1 tablespoon fresh Italian parsley (flat leaf)
¾ to 1 teaspoon fresh garlic, crushed
⅛ teaspoon salt
⅛ teaspoon freshly ground pepper

Serves 10 to 15.

Beat cream cheese in large mixing bowl until softened. Add butter, beating until thoroughly mixed. Gradually beat in cream until smooth. Add remaining ingredients, stirring until thoroughly mixed. Pack into 3 cup crock or attractive container. Refrigerate covered until firm, 4 to 6 hours. Stand at room temperature one hour before serving.

Serve with toast points or crisp crackers (unsalted are the best). Can be stored in refrigerator up to one week.

PADILLO

A wonderful version of a popular Mexican salsa. This is best when made with garden-fresh tomatoes.

4 large tomatoes
13-ounce can black olives, drained
13-ounce can green chiles, drained
4 green onions, chopped
6 tablespoons oil
3 tablespoons wine vinegar
2 teaspoons garlic salt

Serves 8 to 10.

Halve tomatoes. Discard juice and seeds by gently squeezing. Quickly chop in a food processor.

Add remaining ingredients and quickly chop again.

Refrigerate and serve with tortilla chips.

ENGLISH PUB EGGS

An absolute must for your next pre-game tailgate party.

Ginger and Spice Vinegar:
1 tablespoon coarse salt
Fresh ginger, 2¼-inch slices
2 teaspoons allspice berries
1 teaspoon black peppercorns, whole
1-quart malt or cider vinegar
½ cup sugar

Eggs:
12 hard boiled eggs, prepared 10 days before use
1½ cups ginger and spice vinegar
6 allspice berries, whole
2 bay leaves
1 teaspoon peppercorns, whole

Serves 12.

At least 3 weeks ahead, prepare the ginger and spice vinegar. Place salt, ginger, allspice berries and peppercorns in a glass bottle or jar. Combine vinegar and sugar in non-aluminum saucepan and bring to a simmer. Pour into bottle. Cap and seal. Let stand in a cool, dark place.

At least 3 days before serving, shell eggs and pack into 1-quart jar. Bring vinegar to boil in non-aluminum pan and let boil about 10 minutes. Add remaining ingredients to jar and ladle hot vinegar over eggs. Cap tightly. Let cool. Refrigerate for at least 3 days prior to serving. Can be refrigerated for up to 2 weeks.

HOMEMADE JERKY

A hearty and healthy snack that hunters will especially appreciate.

3-pounds lean round or flank of venison, elk or beef, cut 2-inches thick
1 tablespoon salt
1 teaspoon onion powder
1 teaspoon garlic powder
1½ teaspoons pepper
1⅓ cups Worchestershire sauce
1¼ cups soy sauce
1 tablespoon liquid smoke, (optional)

Makes 8 to 12 generous servings.

Trim all fat from meat for better storage quality. Partially freeze and cut meat in thin strips with the grain, about ¼ by ½ by 6-inches. Try to keep meat in uniform size pieces. Put meat in plastic bags. Mix remaining ingredients and pour over meat. Seal bags. Marinate overnight in refrigerator. Drain. Pat dry with paper towels.

Lay jerky close together on oven racks. Line bottom of oven with foil to catch drippings. Turn oven to lowest possible temperature. Leave door open a crack. Dry for about 3½ hours, but avoid over-drying. Jerky should not be crisp. Check often.

Store finished jerky in airtight container. If all fat has been removed jerky will keep indefinitely. May be frozen.

RASPBERRY NOG

1 10-ounce package frozen raspberries
6 large eggs, separated
4 tablespoons sugar
2 6-ounce cans frozen red fruit punch concentrate, thawed and undiluted
¼ cup Cointreau liqueur
1½ cups light rum
3 cups milk
1 cup whipping cream

Makes 3½ quarts.

Purée raspberries in blender, sieve or food mill Beat egg yolks in large bowl. Gradually add two tablespoons sugar and beat until yolks are slightly thickened. Stir in punch concentrate, raspberry purée, Cointreau, rum and milk. Beat egg whites until soft peaks form. Gradually add remaining sugar and beat until stiff peaks form. Fold gently but not thoroughly into punch mixture. Whip cream and fold in. Serve.

THE ULTIMATE MAI TAI

1 cup light rum
1 cup dark rum
½ cup grenadine
½ cup slow gin
¼ cup lemon juice
48 to 96-ounces pineapple juice, to taste
Fresh fruit (pineapple, strawberries, orange wedges)

Serves 8 to 10.

Mix together light and dark rum, grenadine, gin and lemon juice in large container. Add pineapple juice to taste. Serve in tall glass over crushed ice and garnish with fresh fruit.

BRANDY SLUSHES

A refreshing treat — great for summer barbeques.

7 cups boiling water
3 cups sugar
3 teaspoons instant tea
2 cups cold water
1 12-ounce can frozen orange juice concentrate
1½ cups lemon juice
2½ cups brandy
Carbonated lemon-lime soda

Serves 12.

Dissolve sugar in boiling water. Mix tea in cold water. Combine. Add orange juice and lemon juice. Cool. Stir in brandy. Freeze completely. Scoop into tall glasses until ⅔ full. Top with soda and stir gently. Serve.

WHITE SANGRIA

Dazzling in a clear glass pitcher and so refreshing.

¼ cup sugar
½ cup Cointreau liqueur
2 limes, cut in wedges
1 lemon, sliced
1 orange, sliced
1 fifth-sized bottle Washington State dry white wine, chilled
4 fresh pineapple wedges
Ice cubes
1 10-ounce bottle club soda, chilled
Whole strawberries for garnish

Serves 6 to 8.

Combine sugar, Cointreau, limes, lemon and orange slices in glass pitcher. Stir until well-blended. When ready to serve, add wine, pineapple wedges and ice cubes to pitcher. Pour into wine glasses or goblets, top with splash or two of club soda. Garnish with strawberry.

PEACH FUZZ

2 peaches, quartered with peelings left on, chilled
1 6-ounce can frozen lemonade
6-ounces water
6-ounces vodka, chilled

Serves 4.

Combine in blender until smooth. Serve.

SHAKEN BLOODY MARY

Cracked ice or small ice cubes
1 cup plus 2 tablespoons vodka
1½ cups tomato juice
¾ cup canned beef bouillon
¼ cup plus 2 tablespoons lemon juice, freshly squeezed
6 dashes Worcestershire sauce
6 dashes hot-pepper sauce
Celery salt
Freshly ground pepper
6 lime wedges

Makes 6 drinks.

Put ice in glass-bottomed shaker. Add vodka, tomato juice, bouillon, lemon juice and sauces. Add celery salt and pepper to taste. Shake and strain into six 6-ounce stemmed glasses. Squeeze lime juice into each glass before garnishing with the wedge.

HOT CHRISTMAS CRANBERRY PUNCH

A Northwest Christmas tradition.

1 48-ounce can cranberry juice
2 quarts water
¾ cup sugar
1 6-ounce can lemonade concentrate, frozen and undiluted
10 to 12 whole cloves
3 cinnamon sticks or ground cinnamon to taste

Makes 24 5-ounce servings.

Simmer all ingredients together for 30 minutes and serve hot.

BREADS AND BRUNCH

BREADS AND BRUNCH

LEMON CLOUD MUFFINS

Light and fluffy with the special "bite" of tart lemon.

½ cup butter or margarine, softened
½ cup sugar
Grated zest of 1 lemon (about 1 tablespoon)
2 tablespoons milk
2 eggs, separated
3 tablespoons fresh lemon juice
1 cup all-purpose or unbleached flour
1 teaspoon baking powder
¼ teaspoon salt

Topping:
¼ cup pecans, finely chopped
1 tablespoon sugar
½ teaspoon nutmeg

Makes 12 muffins.

Preheat oven to 375°. Grease 12 muffin cups or use paper liners.

Cream butter, sugar, lemon zest, milk, and egg yolks until light and fluffy. Beat in lemon juice.

Combine dry ingredients and stir into creamed mixture just until blended.

Beat egg whites to soft peaks and fold into batter.

Spoon into prepared muffin cups.

Combine topping ingredients and sprinkle over each muffin.

Bake in preheated oven for 15 to 20 minutes or until lightly browned.

LEMON YOGURT MUFFINS

Certain to become a family favorite, these delicate muffins easily disappear.

2 cups all-purpose flour
1 teaspoon baking soda
1 teaspoon baking powder
¼ teaspoon salt
¼ cup sugar
2 tablespoons honey
2 large eggs, room temperature
1¼ cups plain yogurt
¼ cup butter, melted and cooled
1 tablespoon fresh lemon rind, grated

Lemon Syrup:
⅓ cup fresh lemon juice
⅓ cup sugar
3 tablespoons water

Makes 12 muffins.

In a small bowl, stir together the flour, baking soda, baking powder, and salt. Mix well. In a large bowl mix together the sugar, honey, eggs, yogurt, melted butter and rind. Add flour mixture and stir just until all ingredients are combined. (Do not over mix.) Divide batter among 12 buttered ½ cup muffin tins. Bake in the middle of a 375° oven for 15 to 20 minutes until pale golden brown and a tester muffin comes out clean.

Make lemon syrup while muffins bake. To prepare syrup, in a heavy saucepan combine the lemon juice, sugar and water. Bring mixture to a boil and boil for 1 minute.

When muffins come out of the oven leave in the pan and pierce the top of each muffin gently 2 or 3 times with a fork. Drizzle 2 or 3 teaspoons of the lemon syrup over each muffin. Let muffins cool in the pan for 3 minutes. Turn out onto a rack to continue cooling.

BREAKFAST PUFFS

So delicious and easy to prepare — calls for ingredients already on your shelf.

Muffins:
⅓ cup shortening, softened
½ cup sugar
1 egg
1½ cups flour
1½ teaspoons baking powder
½ teaspoon salt
¼ teaspoon nutmeg
½ cup milk

Topping:
⅓ cup butter, melted
½ cup sugar
1 teaspoon cinnamon

Makes 12 muffins.

Preheat oven to 350°. Cream shortening, sugar and egg together. Sift together next 4 dry ingredients. Stir dry ingredients into creamed mixture, alternating with milk.

Fill greased muffin tins ⅔ full. (Do not use paper muffin cups.) Bake 20 to 25 minutes, until golden brown.

Remove from oven. Immediately roll in melted butter, then in mixture of sugar and cinnamon.

BLUEBERRY SQUARE MUFFINS

A sweet variation on the traditional blueberry muffin.

Filling:
½ cup graham cracker crumbs
½ cup brown sugar, firmly packed
1 teaspoon cinnamon

Batter:
½ cup margarine
1 cup sugar
1 cup sour cream
1 teaspoon vanilla
3 eggs
2 cups flour
1 teaspoon baking soda
½ teaspoon salt

Topping:
2 cups blueberries, fresh, frozen, or canned
1 tablespoon flour
Powdered sugar

Serves 15.

Grease and flour 9 by 13-inch pan. Combine all filling ingredients, set aside.

Combine margarine, sugar, sour cream, vanilla and eggs at low speed until blended. Sift flour, soda, and salt together. Combine and blend into batter. Spread half of the batter in bottom of pan. Sprinkle filling mixture evenly over batter. Spread remaining batter over filling.

In a small bowl, combine blueberries and flour. Toss lightly to coat. Spoon over top of batter. Bake 40 to 50 minutes at 350°. Cool slightly, sprinkle with powdered sugar. Cut into squares.

SWEDISH FRUIT ROLLS

1 cup cottage cheese
3 eggs
1 tablespoon oil
Pinch salt
¼ cup flour

Serves 2 to 4.

Combine all ingredients in a blender or food processor. Mix until smooth. Cook on lightly oiled, preheated griddle, as 4 to 5-inch pancakes. Serve with fresh berries or jam.

LEMONY RICOTTA PANCAKES

Let the light, lemony flavor brighten your morning.

¾ cup all-purpose flour
1 teaspoon baking powder
½ teaspoon salt
½ teaspoon ground nutmeg
2 beaten eggs
1 cup ricotta cheese
½ cup milk
1 tablespoon sugar
½ teaspoon lemon peel, finely shredded
1 teaspoon lemon juice
Jam, preserves or powdered sugar

Serves 2 to 4.

In a large mixing bowl stir together flour, baking powder, salt and nutmeg. Set aside. In a medium mixing bowl stir together eggs and ricotta cheese. Stir in milk, sugar, lemon peel and lemon juice. Add to the flour mixture all at once. Stir just until blended. For each pancake, pour about ⅓ cup of the batter onto a hot, lightly greased griddle or heavy skillet. Spread the batter into a 5-inch circle. Cook till pancakes are golden brown, turning to cook other side when pancakes have a bubbly surface and slightly dry edges, 1½ to 2 minutes per side. Serve immediately with jam, preserves or sprinkle with powdered sugar.

ROSE ROLLS

These prize-winning sweet rolls are pleasing to both the palate and the eye. Prepare dough the night before serving and bake fresh in the morning.

3¾ to 4¼ cups unsifted flour
½ cup sugar
2 teaspoons salt
2 packages dry yeast
¾ cup milk
½ cup water
½ cup margarine
1 egg, room temperature
1 22-ounce can cherry pie filling

Buttercream Frosting:
1 cup powdered sugar
⅛ teaspoon salt
⅛ cup milk
½ teaspoon vanilla
1½ tablespoons butter or margarine, softened

Makes 18 rolls.

In a large bowl mix 1 cup flour, sugar, salt and undissolved yeast. Combine milk, water and margarine in a saucepan. Heat over low heat until liquids are very warm. Margarine does not need to melt. Gradually add to dry ingredients and beat 2 minutes at medium speed. Add egg and ½ cup flour. Beat at high speed 2 minutes. Add enough additional flour to make stiff batter. Cover bowl tightly with foil. Chill two hours or overnight.

Turn dough out onto lightly floured board; divide into 18 equal pieces. Gently roll each piece to a rope, 15-inches long. Hold one end of each rope in place and wind dough around loosely to form coil, tucking end firmly underneath. Place on greased baking sheets about 2-inches apart. Cover, let rise in a warm place, free from draft, until doubled in bulk; about one hour. Make indentations about 1-inch wide in center of each coil, pressing to bottom. Fill with cherry pie filling.

Bake at 400°, 12 to 15 minutes, or until done. Remove from baking sheets and cool on wire racks.

In a mixing bowl, combine frosting ingredients by beating until smooth. When cool, drizzle on rolls.

ORANGE COCONUT SWEET ROLLS

Start your day with the sweet tropical flavor of these sensational rolls.

Dough:
1 tablespoon or 1 package active dry yeast
¼ cup warm water (110° to 115°)
¼ cup sugar
1 teaspoon salt
2 eggs, slightly beaten
½ cup sour cream
10 tablespoons butter, melted
2¾ to 3 cups all-purpose flour

Filling:
¾ cup sugar
¾ cup shredded coconut, lightly toasted
2 tablespoons grated orange zest

Glaze:
¾ cup sugar
½ cup sour cream
2 tablespoons orange juice
¼ cup butter

Topping:
¼ cup toasted coconut

Makes 24 rolls.

In a large bowl, soften yeast in warm water. When foamy, add sugar, salt, eggs, sour cream, and 6 tablespoons butter. Mix well. Gradually beat in flour to form a stiff dough. Cover and let rise in warm place until doubled.

Combine filling ingredients and set aside.

Punch dough down and knead on floured surface about 2 minutes. Divide dough in half.

Roll each half of dough into a 12-inch circle and brush each circle with 2 tablespoons of the melted butter. Sprinkle each circle with half of the filling mixture. Cut into 12 wedges and roll each wedge up "croissant style" beginning at wide edge.

Place rolls, seam side down, in 3 rows in a greased 9 by 13-inch baking dish. Cover and let rise until doubled in bulk, 20 to 30 minutes.

Bake in preheated 350° oven for 18 to 20 minutes. Remove from oven and leave in pan.

Combine glaze ingredients in saucepan. Bring to a boil and boil for 3 minutes. Pour over rolls in pan. Sprinkle with ¼ cup toasted coconut.

CINNAMON BRIOCHE

The traditional cinnamon roll made elegant. Ideal for brunch or an afternoon tea.

⅓ cup sugar
1-ounce yeast
11 eggs, room temperature
2½ teaspoons salt
2⅔ cups all-purpose flour
2⅔ cups unbleached all-purpose flour
1½ cups butter, room temperature
¾ cup sugar
1½ tablespoons cinnamon
¾ cup walnuts, coarsely ground

Icing:
1 cup powdered sugar
3 tablespoons milk

Makes 12.

In a large bowl of heavy-duty mixer fitted with dough hook, blend ⅓ cup sugar and yeast to paste. Add 9 eggs and salt and mix until just blended. Add flours all at once and mix until dough comes together. Add butter in walnut-size pieces and knead with mixer at medium speed until dough is smooth and elastic, about 15 minutes.

Oil large bowl. Transfer dough to bowl, turning to coat entire surface. Dust top lightly with flour. Cover with plastic wrap. Let rise in warm draft-free area until doubled in volume, about 1 hour.

Punch dough down in bowl. Cover with plastic wrap and refrigerate overnight.

Shape dough into square. Roll out on lightly floured surface into 18 by 31-inch rectangle about ¼-inch thick. Make egg glaze by beating remaining eggs until blended; brush part of glaze lightly over dough. Blend sugar and cinnamon, and sprinkle over top. Sprinkle walnuts over top.

Starting from 1 long edge, roll dough up as for jelly roll. Brush seam with glaze to seal. Cut roll into 12 1½-inch thick slices. Arrange on baking sheets, cut side down, spacing 2-inches apart. Let rise in warm draft-free area until puffed, about 1 hour.

Preheat oven to 425°. Brush rolls with remaining egg glaze. Bake until golden brown, about 15 minutes.

Combine powdered sugar and milk; brush rolls with icing and serve.

LEMON BRIOCHE BRAID

Light as a feather, this lemony brioche melts in your mouth.

1¾ to 2¼ cups flour
¼ cup sugar
¼ teaspoon salt
1 package active dry yeast
¼ cup milk
¼ cup water
⅓ cup butter or margarine
2 eggs, at room temperature
½ teaspoon lemon extract
Butter or margarine, melted

Sugar Glaze:
¾ cup unsifted powdered sugar
1 tablespoon hot water
½ teaspoon lemon extract

Makes 1 coffee cake.

In a large electric mixer bowl thoroughly combine ¾ cup flour, sugar, salt and undissolved yeast. Combine milk, water and ⅓ cup butter or margarine in a small saucepan over low heat, just until warm. Gradually add to dry ingredients and beat 2 minutes at medium speed with electric mixer, scraping the bowl occasionally.

Add eggs, lemon extract and ½ cup flour, or enough flour to make a thick batter. Beat at high speed 2 minutes, scraping the bowl occasionally.

Add enough additional flour to make a stiff batter. Beat by hand for 5 minutes or with a heavy duty electric mixer. Brush the top of the dough with melted butter or margarine. Cover and let rise in a warm place free from draft, until doubled in bulk, about 1 hour.

Stir batter down and cover bowl tightly with foil and refrigerate overnight.

Turn dough out onto a lightly floured surface. Divide dough into 3 pieces. Roll each piece into a 20-inch rope. Braid the ropes together, pinch the ends to seal. Place on a large greased baking sheet. Cover and let rise in a warm place, free from draft, until doubled in bulk, about 1 hour.

Bake at 375° for 20 to 30 minutes, or until golden brown.

To make sugar glaze, combine ingredients and mix until smooth. Remove from baking sheet and frost with sugar glaze. Best when served warm.

GOLDEN EGGNOG BRAID

Dairy-eggnog gives this festive bread its "holiday" appeal. Food processor makes it easy.

2 tablespoons water (105° to 115°F)
2 tablespoons sugar
1 package dry yeast
2½ cups flour
2 tablespoons butter or margarine
1 teaspoon salt
¼ teaspoon ground nutmeg
¾ to 1 cup dairy eggnog, room temperature
Sliced almonds

Makes 1 loaf.

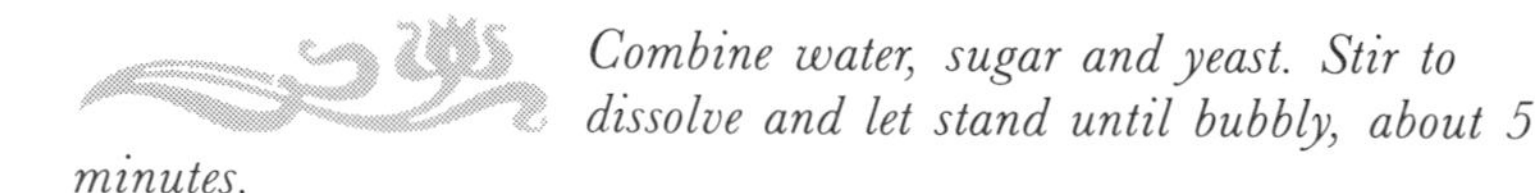

Combine water, sugar and yeast. Stir to dissolve and let stand until bubbly, about 5 minutes.

Fit processor with steel blade. Measure flour, butter, salt and nutmeg into work bowl. Process until mixed, about 15 seconds. Add yeast mixture to flour mixture, process until blended, about 10 seconds.

Turn on processor and very slowly drizzle just enough eggnog through feed tube into flour mixture so dough forms a ball that cleans the sides of the bowl. Process until ball turns around bowl about 25 times. Turn off processor and let dough stand 1 to 2 minutes.

Turn on processor and gradually drizzle in enough remaining eggnog to make a soft dough, smooth and satiny but not sticky. Process until dough turns around bowl about 15 times.

Let dough stand in work bowl 10 minutes. Turn dough onto lightly floured surface and shape into a ball. Place in lightly greased bowl, turn over to grease top, cover loosely with plastic wrap and let stand in warm place until doubled, about 1 hour.

Punch down dough. Let stand 10 minutes. Divide into 3 equal pieces. Shape each piece into a strand 20-inches long. Braid the 3 strands together. Place on greased baking sheet. Brush with oil and let stand in warm place until doubled, about 45 minutes. Brush braid with eggnog and sprinkle with sliced almonds.

Bake at 375° for 25 to 30 minutes. Remove braid from baking sheet and cool on wire rack.

BRAIDED DINNER ROLLS

Liquid Spice Flavoring:
3 cloves
1 bay leaf
½ stick cinnamon
¾ cup water

Bread Dough:
¼ cup warm water (between 110° and 115°)
1 ¼-ounce package active dry yeast
3 tablespoons sugar
2 teaspoons salt
¼ cup plus 1 teaspoon melted butter
¾ cup warm milk
1 large egg, at room temperature
3½ cups sifted all-purpose flour
1 teaspoon liquid spice flavoring
1 egg yolk, lightly beaten with fork
Sesame or poppy seeds

Makes 2 dozen.

Simmer cloves, bay leaf, cinnamon and water, covered, over low heat for about 20 minutes. Strain and reserve liquid.

Rinse a large mixing bowl in warm water. Pour the ¼ cup warm water into bowl and sprinkle on the yeast. Cover with a warm plate and set aside for 15 minutes. Add sugar, salt, ¼ cup melted butter, and warm milk to the yeast and cover. Beat one egg and add to yeast mixture.

Sift flour and liquid spice flavoring slowly into the yeast mixture, stirring until a soft dough is formed. Knead for 15 minutes, with 5 minute rest intervals between each 5 minutes of kneading. Put dough back into bowl and brush lightly with about a teaspoon of melted butter. Cover with a clean dish towel and wrap a bath towel loosely around the bowl. Let dough rise for 1 hour or until double in bulk, in a warm place without drafts.

Divide dough in half. Cut each half into six balls. Roll each ball out onto a floured board into a rectangle about ¼-inch thick. Cut into three strips each about 3½-inches long and ½-inch wide. Take the three strips, press together at one end and braid them. Finish by pressing braids together at other end.

Place on buttered cookie sheets, leaving at least 1½-inches around each roll for rising. Separate egg, beating yolk lightly. Brush dough with egg yolk and sprinkle with sesame or poppy seeds.

Cover cookie sheets with a clean dish towel. Let rolls rise in a warm place for about 45 minutes or until double in bulk.

Bake at 350° for 30 minutes or until a deep golden color. Rolls should be shiny and the color of tea when removed from the oven.

CARDAMOM KNOTS

Grandma's blue ribbon winner!

½ cup butter
6 tablespoons whipping cream
⅓ cup sugar
½ teaspoon salt
½ teaspoon cardamom
1 package active dry yeast
¼ cup warm water, 105° to 115°
4 eggs
About 4 cups all-purpose flour
1 tablespoon cold water

Makes 2 dozen.

In a 1- or 2-quart pan, melt the butter. Remove from heat and stir in the cream, sugar, salt and cardamom. Let cool to lukewarm.

In a large bowl, combine the yeast and warm water. Let stand 5 minutes to soften. Add the cooled butter mixture, 3 eggs, and 2 cups of the flour. Mix until well blended. .Then beat with a mixer at medium speed for 2 minutes. With a heavy-duty mixer or a heavy spoon, gradually stir in approximately 1⅔ cups more flour to make a stiff dough.

Turn dough out onto a board coated with some of the remaining ⅓ cup flour. Knead until smooth and slightly elastic, about 10 minutes. Add more flour as needed to prevent sticking. Place dough in a greased bowl, turning to grease top. Cover bowl with plastic wrap and let dough rise in a warm place until doubled, about 1½ hours.

Punch dough down. Divide into 24 equal balls. Roll each ball into a 6-inch long rope. Twist or tie rope into a knot. Tuck ends under and place on greased baking sheets. Cover sheets with plastic wrap and let rise about 45 minutes until puffy.

Separate remaining egg; beat yolk with 1 tablespoon water. Brush rolls with egg yolk mixture. Bake for 12 to 15 minutes at 375° until golden.

CHEESE-FILLED TORTA

Cut this lovely cheese bread into wedges and serve warm. The dough can be started one day ahead.

Dough:
2 envelopes dry yeast
1 cup warm water (105° to 115°)
½ cup butter, melted
3 eggs
1 tablespoon sugar
1 teaspoon salt
4 cups unbleached all-purpose flour

Filling:
2 tablespoons olive oil
2 small onions, thinly sliced
½ cup red bell pepper, minced
½ cup green bell pepper, minced
½ cup Parmesan cheese, freshly grated
½ teaspoon pepper, coarsely ground or dried red pepper flakes (optional)
1-pound shredded Fontina or Monterey Jack cheese, (about 4 cups)

Glaze:
1 egg beaten with 1 tablespoon milk

Serves 8.

Sprinkle yeast over warm water in large bowl, stirring to dissolve. Let stand 5 minutes. Whisk in butter, eggs, sugar and salt. Add flour 1 cup at a time and mix until smooth dough forms. Cover and refrigerate at least 2 hours. (Can be prepared 1 day ahead.)

Heat oil in heavy, large skillet over low heat. Add onions and bell peppers and cook until onions are translucent, stirring occasionally, about 15 minutes. Cool completely.

Grease 12-inch round pizza pan. Divide dough in half. Roll 1 piece out on lightly floured surface to 12-inch round. Transfer to prepared pan. Press edges to form ½-inch-high rim. Sprinkle dough with Parmesan, then top with onion mixture. Sprinkle with pepper if desired. Cover with Fontina.

Roll remaining dough out on lightly floured surface to 12-inch round. Cut into 1-inch-wide strips. Weave strips atop filling in lattice pattern. Fold rim over strips and pinch to seal. Flute edges. (Can be prepared 5 hours ahead. Cover and refrigerate.) Let dough rise in warm draft-free area for 30 minutes.

Cover with glaze. Bake at 350° for 40 to 45 minutes or until brown.

ONION LOVER'S TWIST

Sweet, tender onions are key to this delectable bread.

1 package dry yeast
¼ cup warm water
4 cups flour
¼ cup sugar
1½ teaspoons salt
½ cup hot water
½ cup milk
¼ cup butter or margarine, softened
1 egg

Filling:
¼ cup butter or margarine
1 cup finely chopped onion or
¼ cup instant minced onions
1 tablespoon grated Parmesan cheese
1 tablespoon sesame or poppy seed
¼ teaspoon garlic powder
¾ teaspoon salt
1 teaspoon paprika

Makes 1 large loaf.

Grease cookie sheet. In a large bowl dissolve yeast in warm water. Add 2 cups flour, sugar, salt, water, milk, butter and egg. With electric mixer, blend at low speed until moistened. Beat 2 minutes at medium speed. By hand, stir in remaining flour to form a soft dough. Cover and let rise in a warm place until light and doubled in size, 45 to 60 minutes.

To prepare filling, melt butter in saucepan and add remaining ingredients.

When dough has doubled in size, stir down and place on a floured board. Knead until no longer sticky. Roll out to an 18 by 12-inch rectangle. Spread with filling, then cut lengthwise into three 18 by 4-inch strips. Beginning with the 18-inch side, roll up each strip. Seal edges and ends. On the prepared cookie sheet braid the three rolls together. Cover and allow to rise until doubled, about 45 to 60 minutes. Bake at 350° for 30 to 35 minutes, or until golden brown. Serve warm or cool.

BEER RYE BREAD

Serve this bread with a variety of cold cuts and gourmet mustards, and let the tailgate party begin!

2 packages dry yeast
½ cup warm water
2½ cups beer
½ cup shortening
1 cup molasses (preferably dark)
1 tablespoon salt
1 tablespoon caraway seeds
5 cups rye flour
4 cups white, all-purpose flour

Glaze:
1 egg
1 tablespoon water

Makes 2 long loaves or 3 round loaves.

Sprinkle dry yeast in warm water. Stir until dissolved. Heat beer until it just starts to bubble. Remove from heat and add shortening. Add molasses, salt and caraway seeds to beer and stir. Cool until lukewarm and stir in dissolved yeast. Beat in rye flour. Beat in white flour until dough is too firm to beat (you may not need it all). Turn out onto floured board. Knead until smooth and elastic, 6 to 10 minutes. Put into greased bowl and butter top of dough. Cover and let rise in warm place until doubled in bulk, about 1½ hours. On a lightly floured board, knead again until smooth. Shape into 2 long loaves or 3 round loaves. Slash top with very sharp knife several times. Brush with egg that has been beaten with 1 tablespoon water. Let loaves stand until doubled in bulk. Brush again with beaten egg. Bake in preheated 350° oven for 40 to 45 minutes.

ELEGANT SANDWICH LOAF

1 loaf unsliced sandwich bread
½ cup butter, softened

Shrimp Salad Filling:
1 hard-cooked egg, chopped
1⅓ cups fresh shrimp, cooked
⅓ cup celery, minced
2 tablespoons lemon juice
¼ teaspoon salt
Dash of pepper
¼ cup mayonnaise

Chicken-Bacon Filling:
8 slices crisp cooked bacon, crumbled
1 cup cooked chicken, finely chopped
¼ cup mayonnaise
1 tablespoon pimento, finely chopped
¼ teaspoon salt
⅛ teaspoon pepper

Cheese Pecan Filling:
3-ounce package cream cheese, softened
1 cup finely chopped pecans
¾ cup or 9-ounce can well-drained crushed pineapple

Frosting:
2 8-ounce packages of cream cheese
½ cup cream
Green food coloring
Peeled cucumber for garnish

Serves 12 to 14.

Trim crusts from unsliced loaf of sandwich bread and cut the loaf into 4 lengthwise slices. Spread one side of each slice with softened butter. Place 1 slice, buttered side up, on a serving platter.

Combine Shrimp Salad Filling ingredients together. Mix well. Spread over bread on the serving platter and top with a second bread slice, buttered side up.

Combine Cheese Pecan Filling ingredients together. Mix well. Spread over second bread slice. Top with third bread slice, buttered side up.

Combine Chicken-Bacon Filling ingredients together. Mix well. Top with remaining bread slice.

To make frosting, mix cream cheese and cream together until smooth. Add food coloring to make a delicate green. Garnish top of loaf with paper-thin slices of peeled cucumber, overlapping slices the entire length. Chill in refrigerator for at least 3 hours or overnight. Serve cold.

HERBED SPONGE ROLL FILLED WITH SHRIMP SALAD

Filling:
4 cups cooked shrimp, chopped
(1½ pounds of cleaned medium shrimp)
¼ cup celery, finely chopped
¼ cup onion, finely chopped
1 tablespoon lemon juice
Salt
Freshly ground black pepper
8 to 10 tablespoons mayonnaise
2 tablespoons fresh dill, finely chopped
2 tablespoons fresh parsley, finely chopped

Sponge Roll:
1 tablespoon oil
6 eggs, separated
¼ cup sugar
½ cup chicken stock, heated
1¼ cups flour
1½ teaspoons baking powder
Pinch of salt
⅓ cup fresh parsley, chopped
2 tablespoons fresh dill, chopped
2 tablespoons Parmesan cheese, grated

Serves 6 to 8.

Combine all ingredients for filling and chill well.

Oil a 10-inch by 15-inch by 1-inch jellyroll pan. Line with oiled wax paper. Set aside. In mixing bowl, beat egg yolks until light and fluffy. Gradually add sugar and beat until thick and lemon-colored, about 5 minutes. With mixer on low, add the chicken stock. Combine flour, baking powder, salt, parsley and dill and add to egg yolk mixture. Mix just until smooth. Using clean bowl and beaters, beat egg whites until they form stiff peaks. Gently fold into yolk mixture. Pour mixture into prepared pan, spreading evenly. Bake for 12 to 15 minutes at 375° or until golden brown on top. Sprinkle another sheet of wax paper with grated cheese. Loosen the sides of the baked sponge roll along the long edges of the pan and invert onto wax paper. Carefully peel off wax paper from bottom of cake.

Spread chilled filling evenly over the sponge roll. Roll up jellyroll fashion starting at the narrow end. Carefully cut into 1-inch slices and serve immediately.

SUNRISE HASH

Serve with Orange Coconut Sweet Rolls, lean ham and a fresh fruit platter for an outstanding Sunday brunch.

8 small potatoes
8 eggs, beaten
8-ounces sour cream
1 medium onion, grated
Fresh green pepper, chopped
Fresh red pepper, chopped
1 teaspoon Beau Monde seasoning
½ teaspoon herbs
½ cup butter, melted
8-ounces fresh mushrooms, sliced
5-ounces dried beef, sliced into narrow strips
8-ounces Swiss cheese, grated
8-ounces Monterey Jack cheese, grated

Serves 4 to 6.

The night before, peel potatoes. Cover with water. Refrigerate overnight.

Butter 3-quart casserole. Beat eggs in large mixing bowl. Add sour cream and seasonings. Grate potatoes and add with remaining ingredients to egg and sour cream mixture, except cheese. Bake at 350° for 30 minutes. Remove. Top with blended cheese. Bake 30 minutes more. For best results, bake in middle of oven.

ASPARAGUS AND EGG CASSEROLE

Tender asparagus makes this casserole a real company pleaser. Serve with lightly browned slices of country ham.

1 pound fresh asparagus
4 tablespoons butter or margarine
4 tablespoons flour
1 cup milk
¾ to 1 cup chicken broth
½ teaspoon dry mustard
⅛ teaspoon onion powder
Dash Worcestershire sauce
Dash white pepper
6 hardcooked eggs, sliced
6-ounces sharp Cheddar cheese, grated

Serves 4.

Lightly grease ovenproof dish. Lightly steam asparagus. Uncover pan and set aside. Melt butter or margarine in medium saucepan. Stir in flour to make roux. Cook over medium-low heat 1 to 2 minutes. Add milk gradually, stirring constantly. As it thickens, add chicken broth, dry mustard, onion powder, Worcestershire sauce and white pepper. Stir until thick and smooth.

Place half of asparagus in greased casserole. Cover with half of eggs. Repeat and pour sauce over all.

Top with grated cheese.

Bake at 350° for 30 minutes.

SALADS

SALADS

MANDARIN GREEN SALAD

A refreshing green salad — caramelized almonds and mandarin oranges add surprising interest. Can be done the day before, and tossed together before serving.

Dressing:
½ teaspoon salt
Pepper to taste
2 tablespoons sugar
2 tablespoons vinegar
¼ cup vegetable oil
4 to 5 drops tabasco sauce
1 tablespoon dried parsley flakes

Salad:
¼ cup almonds, whole or sliced
2 tablespoons sugar
½ head romaine lettuce
½ head red-leaf lettuce
1 cup celery, chopped
2 to 3 green onions, thinly sliced
1 11-ounce can mandarin orange segments, drained

Serves 6.

To make dressing, combine all ingredients in a jar. Cover and shake vigorously. Refrigerate until ready to use.

To make salad, caramelize the almonds by combining almonds and sugar in a teflon coated frypan. Cook over medium heat until sugar melts. Stir constantly to coat almonds well. When a nice rich caramel color is reached set pan aside to cool. Break almonds apart and store in covered jar until ready to use.

Wash and dry the lettuce and tear into bite-size pieces. Combine with celery and green onion. Toss lightly. If you're making this the day before, the greens should be kept in a large plastic bag in the refrigerator.

To assemble salad before serving, combine salad greens, caramelized almonds, mandarin orange segments, drained, and dressing. Toss well.

SALAD GREENS WITH HAZELNUTS

Be adventurous in your choice of fresh, good-quality salad greens.

1 medium shallot, minced
1 medium clove garlic, minced
1 tablespoon balsamic vinegar
Salt and freshly ground pepper
6 tablespoons olive oil (preferably extra-virgin)
1 medium Granny Smith apple, cored and julienned
6 cups torn salad greens, (combine mild and bitter greens such as green leaf, romaine and butter lettuce, kale, arugula, sorrel, watercress and radicchio)
3 tablespoons hazelnuts, toasted, husked and chopped
Fresh chives, snipped fine

Makes 6 servings.

Squeeze shallot in towel to remove bitter juices. Place in small bowl. Add garlic, vinegar, salt and pepper and mix well. Gradually whisk in oil in thin stream. Add apple.

Combine greens in large bowl. Pour apple mixture over and toss well. Garnish with hazelnuts and chives.

SWEET AND SOUR SALAD

1 head romaine lettuce
1 head red-leaf lettuce
1 bunch spinach (about ½ pound)
2 cups canned mandarin orange segments, drained
1½ cups feta cheese, crumbled
½ pound bacon, cooked, drained, and crumbled
½ medium red onion, sliced in rings

Dressing:
¼ cup sugar
1 teaspoon grated onion
1 teaspoon dry mustard
1 teaspoon salt
⅓ cup cider vinegar
1 cup vegetable oil
1½ teaspoon poppy seeds
1 teaspoon sesame seeds

Serves 8.

Combine lettuce and spinach leaves, orange segments, cheese, bacon, and red onion slices. In another bowl, combine sugar, grated onion, mustard, salt, and vinegar and blend with a whisk. Add oil gradually, blending well. Stir in poppy seeds and sesame seeds and toss salad with dressing. Serve immediately.

THE ULTIMATE CAESAR SALAD

Caesar salad takes a spectacular turn with Romano cheese and bacon.

Salad:
2 tablespoons oil
Salt
1 large clove garlic
2 tomatoes, cut in eighths
1 large head romaine
¼ cup green onion, chopped
½ cup fresh Romano cheese, grated
1 pound bacon, fried crisp and chopped
1 cup croutons, optional

Dressing:
⅓ cup olive oil
⅓ cup lemon juice
¾ teaspoon fresh mint, chopped or
¼ teaspoon dried mint
¼ teaspoon fresh ground black pepper
¼ teaspoon oregano
1 coddled egg

Serves 6.

In large bowl, place 2 tablespoons oil, sprinkle with salt and rub bowl firmly with cut piece of garlic. Place tomato pieces in bottom of bowl. Add torn romaine, onion, cheese, bacon and croutons.

To make dressing, combine all remaining ingredients except egg. Place egg in boiling water, turn off heat and let stand 1 minute. Crack, add to oil mixture and whip vigorously. Toss with salad and serve immediately.

ASPARAGUS VINAIGRETTE

These crispy asparagus spears are seasoned with a zesty vinaigrette. So easy to prepare and especially nice to have on hand for drop-in guests.

2-pounds asparagus, cooked and cooled
¾ cup olive oil
¼ cup red wine vinegar
1 teaspoon salt
½ teaspoon black pepper
2 teaspoons green onion, chopped
1 tablespoon capers
2 tablespoons stuffed green olives, chopped
¼ teaspoon thyme

Serves 6.

Cook asparagus for 2 to 3 minutes in boiling water until tender-crisp. Cool immediately under cold, running water. Mix remaining ingredients and pour over asparagus.

Chill for 24 hours before serving.

BROCCOLI AND CAULIFLOWER SALAD

Dressing:
½ cup sugar
2 tablespoons vinegar
1 6-ounce can evaporated milk

Salad:
1 large bunch broccoli, cut up, about 2 pounds
1 head cauliflower, cut up
1 large onion, sliced

Serves 6.

Mix dressing ingredients. Pour over vegetables. Cover and refrigerate for at least 6 hours.

BACON AND CAULIFLOWER SALAD

This new and tantalizing salad is a pleasant change from routine green salads.

Dressing:
1 cup mayonnaise
3 tablespoons lemon juice
1 tablespoon prepared mustard
1 tablespoon basil
⅛ teaspoon ground nutmeg

Salad:
1 pound sliced bacon
1 medium cauliflower
1 small red onion, finely chopped
Pepper
Lettuce leaves
3 cups iceberg lettuce, shredded

Serves 4 to 6.

To make dressing, stir together ingredients. Cook bacon until crisp. Drain on paper towels, crumble, and set aside. Break cauliflower into florets and slice thinly. Mix cauliflower with onion, half of bacon and dressing. Add pepper to taste. At this point, salad may be covered and refrigerated overnight to improve flavor. Line a salad bowl with lettuce leaves. Mound shredded lettuce into center. Top with cauliflower mixture and remaining bacon. Serve.

TOMATO AND ROASTED PEPPER SALAD

Colorful, inviting. . . and bursting with flavor. Use a good quality olive oil and red wine vinegar for best results.

Salad:
4 large red peppers, roasted with skins removed
4 large tomatoes, peeled and cut into wedges
10 large ripe, pitted black olives

Dressing:
2 tablespoons olive oil
2 tablespoons red wine vinegar
1 tablespoon parsley, chopped
1 teaspoon ground cumin
1 clove garlic, minced
Chopped parsley for garnish

Serves 6 to 8.

To roast peppers, place on a grill on high heat and blister skins until almost blackened. Or in a 400° oven, blister until skin is blackened and pulling away from meat of pepper. Remove from heat and place damp paper towels over the peppers. Cool and skins are easy to remove.

Slice roasted peppers into ½-inch strips and place in a bowl with tomato wedges and olives.

Combine the dressing ingredients in a jar and pour over salad. Cover and let stand at room temperature about 4 hours. Garnish with extra chopped parsley and serve.

TOMATO MOZZARELLA SALAD

This salad is unsurpassed with vine-ripened, garden fresh tomatoes. A Northwest summer staple.

Vinaigrette:
1 tablespoon prepared Dijon-style mustard
4 tablespoons red wine vinegar
1 teaspoon sugar
½ teaspoon salt
½ teaspoon freshly ground black pepper
Minced parsley or snipped chives
½ cup olive oil

Salad:
4 large ripe tomatoes, cut into ¼-inch slices
2 pounds fresh mozzarella cheese cut into ¼-inch slices, be sure not to use packaged cheese
¼ cup fresh basil, chopped
¼ cup Italian parsley, chopped
½ cup black olives, sliced
½ cup vinaigrette
Freshly ground black pepper

Serves 6.

To prepare vinaigrette, measure mustard into bowl. Whisk in vinegar, sugar, salt, pepper and herbs. Continue to whisk mixture slowly, dribbling in olive oil until mixture thickens. Add seasonings to taste. Cover until ready to use and, if necessary, whisk again. Vinaigrette is best if made just before serving.

Alternate overlapping slices of tomato and mozzarella on a large platter. Sprinkle basil, parsley and black olives over slices. Immediately before serving, drizzle vinaigrette over salad and add black pepper to taste. Serve at room temperature.

OVERNIGHT CABBAGE SLAW

A fresh version of the delicatessen regular.

Slaw:
½ medium red or green cabbage, shredded
1 small sweet onion, sliced thinly
(white or red depending on cabbage color)
½ medium green pepper, diced
2 medium carrots, sliced in thin rounds

Dressing:
⅔ cup vinegar
⅓ cup vegetable oil
¼ cup brown sugar
1 teaspoon salt
¼ teaspoon pepper

Serves 4.

Combine vegetables in large salad bowl. Mix dressing in bottle or covered container. Shake until mixed well. Pour over salad, mix until well coated. Cover and refrigerate at least 8 hours before serving.

At serving time, stir thoroughly, then drain.

Add Italian dressing for stronger taste.

MOROCCAN VEGETABLE SALAD

Superb with lavash — the Greek cracker bread — or whole wheat crackers.

Salad:
½-pound small whole mushrooms
1½ cups cooked garbanzo beans
1 cup pitted large black olives
2 cups green olives
¾ cup green onions, coarsely chopped
2 green peppers, chopped
2 red peppers, chopped
1 dozen cherry tomatoes

Dressing:
1 cup plain yogurt
½ cup mayonnaise
2 cloves garlic, mashed
2 tablespoons olive oil
1 tablespoon lemon juice
1 teaspoon powdered cumin
⅛ teaspoon turmeric (or curry)
Salt and freshly ground pepper

Lettuce leaves

Serves 4 to 5.

To make salad, steam mushrooms 5 minutes; cool. Combine with remaining ingredients and chill 2 hours. To make dressing, mix all ingredients and chill 2 hours. Just before serving, lightly coat mushroom mixture with dressing. Serve on lettuce leaves. Pass remaining dressing.

HERBED POTATO SALAD

Deceptively simple, this potato salad has a flavor all its own.

3-pounds potatoes
1 teaspoon salt
1 teaspoon white pepper, freshly ground
1 teaspoon dry mustard
1 teaspoon garlic, finely minced
¼ cup apple cider vinegar
½ cup olive or avocado oil
½ cup plain yogurt
¼-pound small sweet onions, sliced thin
4 tablespoons fresh basil, finely chopped
3 tablespoons fresh chives or scallion tops, finely chopped
2 tablespoons fresh dill leaves, finely snipped
1 cucumber, sliced

Serves 4 to 6.

Wash potatoes. Steam until just tender, but not soft. While the potatoes are steaming, prepare salad dressing. In a small bowl, combine the salt, pepper, dry mustard and garlic. Whisk in vinegar. In a slow steady stream, whisk in oil until the mixture is smooth and thick. Whisk in yogurt. The dressing will be thinner after the yogurt is added. Pour ⅓ of dressing into large shallow dish and set aside.

Remove potatoes from heat and drain. Peeling potatoes is optional. Place the whole potatoes into the dish with dressing. Let them cool briefly, about 5 minutes. Cut the potatoes in ¼-inch slices or chunks. Add the onions and the dressing. Toss thoroughly. Add the herbs and toss once again. Transfer to salad bowl or platter and serve at room temperature.

DILLY POTATO-ASPARAGUS SALAD

Pickled asparagus and red potatoes set this salad apart.

6 to 8 cups water
1 teaspoon salt
1 teaspoon caraway seed
2½ to 3 pounds red potatoes
2 16-ounce jars pickled asparagus, drained, reserving ¾ cup juice
1 teaspoon sugar
1 teaspoon lemon pepper
1 teaspoon salt
2 teaspoons dried dill, or 2 tablespoons fresh dill
⅛ teaspoon tarragon
1 tablespoon mustard
4 tablespoons oil
2 small onions, finely chopped
3 green onions, finely chopped
1 red bell pepper, finely chopped

Serves 8 to 10.

Bring water, salt and caraway seed to a boil. Add whole potatoes and cook until tender.

To prepare marinade, put ¾ cup juice from canned asparagus into mixing bowl. Add sugar, lemon pepper, salt, dill, tarragon, mustard and oil. Mix together.

Drain remaining juice from asparagus and cut asparagus into pieces, setting aside 1½-inch tips. Cut up the garlic clove from the can. Add asparagus, except tips, and garlic to marinade. Stir in onions, green onions and pepper.

While potatoes are still hot, peel and slice. Cut into cubes and fold in small batches, into marinade. Let sit 2 to 3 hours. After mixture has cooled, it can be refrigerated.

Garnish with asparagus tips.

HAWAIIAN POTATO SALAD

A potato salad with a tropical flair — ideal for your next barbeque.

2-pounds salad potatoes
½ cup green pepper, chopped
½ cup celery, chopped
¼ cup parsley, chopped
¼ cup cucumber, diced
1 cup fresh pineapple, chopped or
1 small can pineapple chunks, drained
¾ cup green onions, sliced
¾ cup salted peanuts

Dressing:
½ cup mayonnaise
½ cup sour cream
1 tablespoon peanut butter, chunky preferred
1 teaspoon curry powder
2 tablespoons vinegar
6 slices crisp bacon, crumbled

Serves 8.

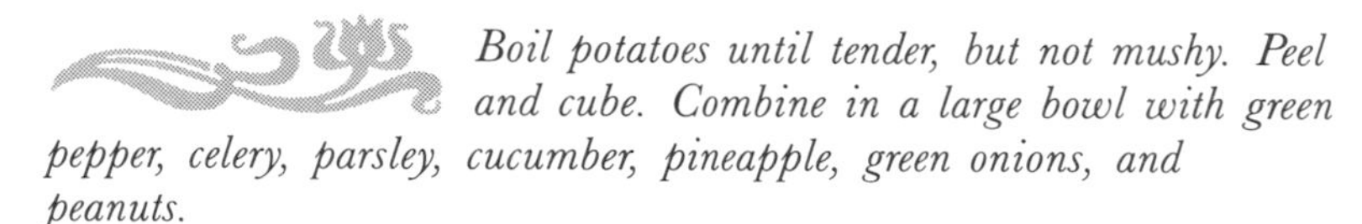

Boil potatoes until tender, but not mushy. Peel and cube. Combine in a large bowl with green pepper, celery, parsley, cucumber, pineapple, green onions, and peanuts.

Combine mayonnaise and sour cream. Add peanut butter and curry powder. Mix well with vinegar. Pour mixture over the other ingredients and blend gently and thoroughly. Refrigerate for at least 1 hour.

Top with crumbled bacon just before serving.

PASTA SALAD WITH SHRIMP

This spectacular salad is wonderful as a luncheon entree or as a cool main course on a hot summer night.

1 12-ounce package tri-colored rotini pasta
1 cup olive oil
1 cup raspberry vinegar
2 teaspoons sugar
½ cup lemon juice
2 teaspoons oregano, crushed
2 teaspoons basil, crushed
1 teaspoon thyme, crushed
1 teaspoon salt
Freshly ground white pepper to taste
1 teaspoon rosemary, crushed
1 teaspoon parsley, crushed
2 teaspoons onion, grated
1 cup broccoli florets
2 carrots, diagonally sliced
1 6-ounce jar marinated artichoke hearts
1 pound baby shrimp, cooked
1 cup freshly grated Parmesan cheese
Fresh parsley for garnish

Serves 8 to 10.

Cook pasta in boiling, salted water until al dente. Rinse and drain.

Combine oil, vinegar, sugar, lemon juice and spices. Mix well. Add to pasta along with vegetables, artichokes in marinade, and shrimp. Mix in thoroughly. Refrigerate, mixing occasionally until ready to serve.

Just before serving, add Parmesan cheese and garnish with fresh parsley.

SEAFOOD PASTA SALAD

Try this versatile dill, parsley, and basil flavored dressing on green salads too.

Fresh Basil-Dill Dressing:
1 egg
¼ cup wine vinegar
½ teaspoon salt
¼ teaspoon pepper
1 clove garlic, peeled and chopped
½ teaspoon sugar
2 tablespoons fresh parsley leaves
2 tablespoons fresh dill weed or
2 to 3 teaspoons dried dill weed
6 to 8 fresh basil leaves, washed
1 cup salad oil

Salad:
1 6½-ounce can snow crabmeat or
1 cup combined fresh crabmeat and tiny shrimp
½-pound spiral macaroni
¼-pound fresh snow peas, washed and blanched
or ½ package frozen peas, thawed
1½ cups fresh broccoli florets,
chopped fine and blanched
1 cup cherry tomatoes, cleaned and halved
⅓ cup water chestnuts, drained and sliced

Serves 4.

To prepare dressing, place all ingredients except oil in blender container. Blend at speed recommended for making mayonnaise, until smooth. With motor running, add oil in pencil-thin stream until mixture thickens. Once it thickens, the remaining oil may be added more rapidly. Set aside.

To prepare salad, drain and flake canned crab or fresh crab, removing cartilage. Rinse shrimp.

Cook macaroni until tender. Drain well and mix in a large bowl with some of the basil-dill dressing while still warm.

Prepare vegetables. Add to macaroni along with seafood. Toss to combine well. Add more dressing to moisten salad to taste. Chill at least ½ hour to 1 hour before serving.

PROSCIUTTO-PASTA SALAD

A hearty main course salad of pasta, artichokes and meat.

Salad:
16-ounces spaghetti twists or bow ties, cooked and drained
2 6-ounce jars marinated artichoke hearts, quartered with marinade reserved for dressing
1 8½-ounce can unmarinated artichoke hearts, drained and quartered
1 8-ounce can pitted black olives, sliced
8-ounces prosciutto, thinly sliced and cut in julienne strips
2 cups frozen tiny peas, thawed and drained

Dressing:
1 cup minced chives or green onions with tops and bottoms
¼ cup lemon juice
⅛ cup olive oil
2 tablespoons minced fresh oregano or 1 tablespoon dried oregano
1 teaspoon garlic salt
Salt to taste
Freshly ground pepper to taste

Serves 10 to 12.

Combine salad ingredients in a large serving bowl.

To prepare dressing, combine ingredients, add reserved marinade and mix well. Pour over salad and toss gently. Serve at room temperature.

IMPERIAL CHICKEN SALAD

Rave reviews will tell you this salad is worthy of its extra preparation time.

⅓ cup sherry
¼ cup soy sauce
5 to 6 fresh ginger, thinly sliced
2 large whole chicken breasts, boned and halved
Salt to taste
Water chestnut flour or cornstarch
Oil for deep frying
½ medium head iceberg lettuce, shredded
6 green onions, chopped
1 bunch fresh coriander (cilantro)
½ cup toasted almonds, chopped
¼ cup toasted sesame seeds
2 to 3-ounces rice sticks or bean threads
½ cup salad oil (not olive oil)
2 tablespoons lemon juice
4 teaspoons soy sauce
2 to 3 teaspoons sesame oil
2 teaspoons dry mustard
2 teaspoons sugar
1 teaspoon fresh ginger, grated
¾ to 1 teaspoon hot pepper or chili oil

Serves 4 to 6 for a main course or 8 for lunch or as a side dish.

Combine sherry, soy and ginger in a medium bowl. Add chicken, cover and refrigerate several hours or overnight, turning chicken once. Drain and pat dry. Lightly salt chicken and coat pieces in flour or cornstarch. (Water chestnut flour makes chicken very crisp and flavorful.) Refrigerate at least 1 hour to allow flour to set.

In large skillet, heat about 2-inches of oil to 375°. Add chicken and deep fry until quite golden and crisp, about 5 minutes per side. Drain on paper towels and let cool.

Slice chicken, including skin, into bite size shreds and place in a large bowl. Add lettuce, onion and coriander. Sprinkle with almonds and sesame seeds.

Preheat oil to 375°. Add rice sticks or bean threads, a handful at a time, and cook quickly. They should immediately explode into a froth of crisp threads. Turn them over so the other side explodes as well. Drain on paper towels before adding to the salad.

Mix together remaining ingredients. Add to salad. Toss and serve.

CURRIED CHICKEN RICE SALAD

Curry adds an exotic note to this highly recommended chicken salad.

3 cups cooked white rice
2 cups cooked chicken or turkey,
cut into 1¼ by ½ by ½-inch strips
1 cup celery, sliced
⅓ cup green onions including tops, sliced
⅔ cup mayonnaise
½ cup chutney, chopped
1 tablespoon curry powder
½ teaspoon salt
¼ cup toasted almonds, slivered
Lettuce

Serves 4 to 6.

Combine rice, chicken or turkey, celery and green onions in mixing bowl. In another bowl, combine mayonnaise, chutney, curry powder and salt, mixing well. Stir into rice mixture. Chill. Sprinkle with almonds and serve on lettuce.

TROPICAL CHICKEN SALAD

Accompany with a cool and uncomplicated wine and crusty bread for an undemanding, elegant luncheon.

Salad:
3 cups cooked chicken, diced
1 cup celery, diced
3 tablespoons green onion, chopped
2 tablespoons lemon juice
1 tablespoon orange juice concentrate
1 8-ounce can pineapple chunks, drained
1 small can mandarin oranges, drained
⅔ cup slivered almonds, toasted

Dressing:
¼ cup mayonnaise
¼ cup sour cream
½ teaspoon lemon peel, grated
1 teaspoon orange peel, grated
1 teaspoon salt
¼ teaspoon chervil, optional

Salad greens

Serves 6.

Combine chicken with celery and onions. Mix in the lemon and orange juices. Chill for several hours.

Just before serving, add pineapple, mandarin oranges and almonds.

For dressing, combine ingredients. Mix gently into salad. Spoon into a bowl lined with greens.

MINTED CHICKEN SALAD WITH FRUIT

Fresh mint is the secret to this lean and healthful chicken salad.

3½ tablespoons vegetable oil
2 teaspoons fresh ginger root, minced
1 teaspoon minced garlic
¼ teaspoon hot red pepper flakes, crushed
1 pound skinless, boneless chicken breasts, cut in 1-inch pieces
½ teaspoon salt
Freshly ground black pepper
⅓ cup chicken stock or water
¼ cup fresh mint, chopped
¼ cup mayonnaise
¼ cup plain yogurt
1 tablespoon lemon juice
1¼ teaspoon lemon zest
½ cantaloupe, cut in 1-inch pieces
1 cup grapes
1 banana or substitute other fruits
⅓ cup sliced scallions
Fresh mint leaves

Serves 4 to 6.

In a large skillet or wok, heat oil. Add 1 teaspoon ginger root, ½ teaspoon garlic and red pepper. Cook over medium-high heat for 10 seconds. Add chicken and stir fry until just cooked through, about 2 minutes. Transfer to a sieve placed over a bowl to catch any juices. Season chicken with salt and pepper to taste. Add chicken stock, 1 tablespoon of mint and any juices from chicken to skillet. Boil over high heat until reduced to about 1 tablespoon, scraping bottom of pan to loosen any brown bits. Strain reduced liquid into a medium bowl and let cool slightly. Stir in mayonnaise, yogurt, lemon juice and zest, remainder of ginger root, garlic and mint. Toss cooled chicken with dressing. Add fruit and scallions and toss gently. Place in serving dish and cover. Refrigerate for at least 2 hours to allow flavors to meld. Serve at room temperature, garnished with fresh mint sprigs.

SHRIMP LIONETTI

Easy, elegant, and delicious. . . prepare by morning and serve by night.

1 cup mayonnaise
¼ cup pesto sauce
1 clove garlic, crushed
1 tablespoon capers, chopped
1-pound small shrimp, cooked and cleaned
1 cup pineapple tidbits, well drained
1 avocado, chopped into ½-inch pieces

Serves 6.

Blend first four ingredients. Add shrimp and pineapple and mix. Add avocado and toss gently. Chill several hours. Serve on individual salad plates lined with red-leaf lettuce. Garnish with thin lemon slice and parsley sprigs.

BEEF SALAD WITH ASPARAGUS AND BROCCOLI

Salad:
1 small flank steak
4 cups fresh asparagus, diagonally sliced into 2-inch pieces
1 bunch broccoli, cut into bite-sized florets

Ginger Dressing:
⅓ cup light soy sauce
¼ cup white vinegar
3 tablespoons sesame oil
1 1½-inch piece fresh ginger, peeled and grated
1 teaspoon sugar
White pepper to taste

Serves 4.

Broil or pan fry flank steak to desired doneness. Cool and slice.

Bring large pot of salted water to rapid boil. Add asparagus and blanch 30 seconds. Remove with slotted spoon and set aside to cool. Add broccoli to the same water and blanch 30 seconds. Drain well and let cool.

Combine all ingredients for dressing. When ready to serve, toss beef slices with dressing. Add vegetables and toss again. Serve at room temperature.

PEAR AND ARTICHOKE SALAD

The refreshing sweetness of pears adds a unique twist to this flavorful salad. Pears, once considered a delicacy for royalty only, are commonplace in the Northwest with its rich, volcanic soil.

1 16-ounce can artichoke hearts
2 ripe pears, chopped
½ cup Italian dressing
2 tablespoons green onion, sliced
2 tablespoons pimento
2 green olives, sliced

Serves 4.

Toss ingredients together and serve on a bed of lettuce.

BLUEBERRY SALAD WITH MINT DRESSING

The mint-flavored dressing brings out the fresh fruit flavor. Blueberries, avocado and cantaloupe add beautiful color.

Mint Dressing:
1 cup sour cream
1 tablespoon sugar
1 tablespoon lime juice
2 tablespoons fresh mint, finely chopped or
1 teaspoon dried mint

Blueberry Salad:
1 avocado, peeled and cubed
1 tablespoon lime juice
1 pint blueberries
1 medium cantaloupe, peeled and cubed

Serves 6 to 8.

Make dressing first. In a small bowl, combine all ingredients. Set aside.

To prepare salad, toss avocado with lime juice in a medium bowl. Add blueberries and cantaloupe. Toss. Serve fruit topped with mint dressing.

MINTED GRAPES IN MELON HALVES

A sensational, sweet salad. Serve with cheese bread sticks or warmed corn muffins.

4 cups seedless grapes or seeded and halved grapes
1 tablespoon fresh mint, minced
1 cup yogurt
2 tablespoons honey
½ teaspoon ginger, grated
2 medium melons (not watermelon), halved, seeded, unchilled

Serves 4.

Toss grapes with mint. Chill well.

Mix yogurt, honey and ginger in blender. Fold into grapes. Heap grape mixture into melon halves.

Serve with cheese bread sticks or warmed corn muffins.

WHITE WINE FRUIT SALAD

2 tablespoons sugar
½ cup dry white wine
1½ teaspoons lemon rind, grated
2 tablespoons fresh lemon juice
4 cups honeydew balls or cubes
4 cups cantaloupe balls or cubes
1 cup seedless green grapes
Lettuce

Serves 8 to 10.

In a shallow serving bowl, dissolve sugar in mixture of wine, lemon rind and lemon juice, stirring constantly. Gently add fruit. Chill two hours tossing occasionally. Drain and serve on a bed of lettuce.

BLUE-BLUE CHEESE DRESSING

This exquisite dressing gains flavor with age.

1 quart mayonnaise
2 cups blue cheese, crumbled
½ cup buttermilk
½ cup sour cream
3 teaspoons Worchestershire sauce
1 small onion, finely chopped
Pepper to taste
½ teaspoon garlic powder

Makes 1½ quarts.

Combine all ingredients. Refrigerate for at least 3 hours.

SOUPS AND CHOWDERS

SOUPS AND CHOWDERS

CHEESE AND BROCCOLI SOUP

Serve with Onion Lover's Twist bread.

3 tablespoons butter
1 small onion, finely chopped
1 small clove garlic, finely chopped
3 tablespoons flour
2 13¾-ounce cans chicken broth
½ cup water
1-pound fresh broccoli
¼ teaspoon leaf thyme, crumbled
¼ teaspoon ground black pepper
1 cup heavy cream
1 egg yolk
1½ cups shredded Swiss cheese
Sliced cherry tomatoes and parsley for garnish

Serves 6.

Melt butter in large saucepan. Add onion and garlic and saute over medium-low heat until onion is tender. Sprinkle flour over mixture and cook, stirring constantly for 3 minutes.

Gradually add broth and water, stirring constantly. Bring to boiling, stirring frequently. Cook broccoli until just tender; coarsely chop. Add broccoli, thyme and pepper to broth mixture. Cover and simmer 3 minutes.

Stir together cream and egg yolk until blended. Stir a little soup into cream mixture. Return to saucepan, stirring to blend. Add cheese. Cook, stirring, until smooth and blended; do not let boil. Serve garnished with tomato and parsley, if desired.

CHEESE SOUP

A beer from one of the Northwest's microbreweries is one of life's finer washes and is splendid with this cheese soup.

6 tablespoons butter or margarine
¾ cup flour
2 cups milk
1 cup cheddar cheese, shredded
3 medium potatoes, thinly sliced
¼ cup green onion, chopped
¼ cup green pepper, chopped
5 cups boiling water
1½ teaspoons chicken bouillon or 2 bouillon cubes
¾ teaspoon salt
Pinch black pepper

Serves 6 to 8.

Melt butter in a saucepan. Add flour, stirring constantly over low heat to form a smooth paste. Gradually add milk, stirring until smooth. Add cheese and remove from heat, stirring occasionally as cheese melts.

In 2-quart saucepan, cook potatoes, onion and green pepper in 5 cups of boiling water until tender. Add chicken bouillon, salt, pepper, and the cheese sauce to the cooked vegetables and water. Mix well and continue cooking over low heat to desired consistency.

BEER AND CHEESE SOUP

A rebirth of cheesemaking in the Northwest is reflected in this hearty soup. Try a cheddar made in the Yakima Valley.

2½ cups beer
2½ tablespoons chicken stock base
1 cup carrot, shredded
1 cup celery, thinly sliced
⅔ cup onion, thinly sliced
3 cups milk
⅓ cup all-purpose flour
1-pound sharp cheddar cheese, shredded
Salt
Freshly ground pepper

Serves 6 to 8.

Combine beer and stock base in 3-quart saucepan and stir over medium-high heat until stock base is dissolved. Add carrot, celery and onion. Cover and simmer until vegetables are tender, about 10 to 12 minutes. Blend 1½ cups milk with flour in medium bowl. Gradually stir into soup, blending well. Add remaining milk and cook, stirring occasionally, until thickened, about 15 minutes. Blend in cheese a little at a time, stirring until melted. Season to taste with salt and pepper. Ladle soup into bowls and serve immediately.

CREAM OF VEGETABLE SOUP

An exquisitely flavored vegetable soup.

¼ cup butter
1½-pounds cauliflower florets, coarsely chopped
1 leek, trimmed and coarsely chopped
1 small white turnip, peeled and coarsely chopped
½ medium onion, coarsely chopped
½ cup peas
1 small carrot, coarsely chopped
1 4-inch piece celery, coarsely chopped
3 cabbage leaves, chopped
4 cups chicken broth, preferably homemade
Salt
Freshly ground pepper
2 boiling potatoes, peeled and coarsely chopped
½ cup whipping cream
2 tablespoons butter, cut into small pieces
Croutons

Serves 6 to 8.

Melt ¼ cup butter in large heavy saucepan over medium heat. Add cauliflower, leek, turnip, onion, peas, carrot, celery and cabbage. Cook 10 minutes, stirring occasionally. Add broth, salt and pepper to taste, and bring to boil. Let boil 10 minutes. Add potatoes and boil until potatoes are tender but not mushy; about 15 minutes. Drain vegetables, reserving broth. Purée vegetables in processor or blender. Return to saucepan with broth. Bring to boil, then remove from heat and whisk in cream and remaining 2 tablespoons butter. Ladle into heated bowls. Garnish with croutons and serve.

CREAM OF CAULIFLOWER SOUP

½ cup onion, chopped
2 tablespoons oil
1 cup celery, chopped
1 medium carrot, shredded finely
1 small head cauliflower, cut in small florets
2 tablespoons parsley, minced and divided
6 cups chicken broth
Bouquet garni (1 small bay leaf, 1 teaspoon tarragon and ½ teaspoon peppercorns tied in triple layer cheesecloth)
¼ cup butter or margarine
¾ cup flour
2 cups milk
1 cup half-and-half
2 teaspoons salt or to taste
1 cup sour cream, at room temperature

Makes about 10 cups.

In Dutch oven cook onion in oil, stirring often, 5 minutes or until tender. Add celery and carrot. Cook 2 minutes stirring often. Stir in cauliflower and 1 tablespoon parsley. Reduce heat to low. Cover and cook 15 minutes, stirring occasionally. Add broth and bouquet garni. Bring to boil over medium heat. Reduce heat. Cover and simmer 5 minutes. Meanwhile melt butter in heavy 2-quart saucepan. Stir in flour to make a thick paste. Beating with wire whisk, gradually add milk. Cook and beat until thickened and smooth. Remove from heat. Stir in half-and-half. Stir sauce into simmering soup. Season with salt and simmer about 15 minutes or until cauliflower is tender, but do not overcook. Just before serving, remove bouquet garni. Mix about ⅓ cup soup into sour cream. Stir sour cream mixture into soup. Reheat. Sprinkle with remaining parsley.

WATERCRESS SOUP

3 large leeks, washed and thinly sliced
2 sweet onions, thinly sliced
1 clove garlic, crushed
¼ cup butter or margarine
4 potatoes, peeled and thinly sliced
6 cups chicken stock or chicken broth
2 bunches watercress
1 cup milk
½ cup heavy cream
Salt and white pepper

Serves 8.

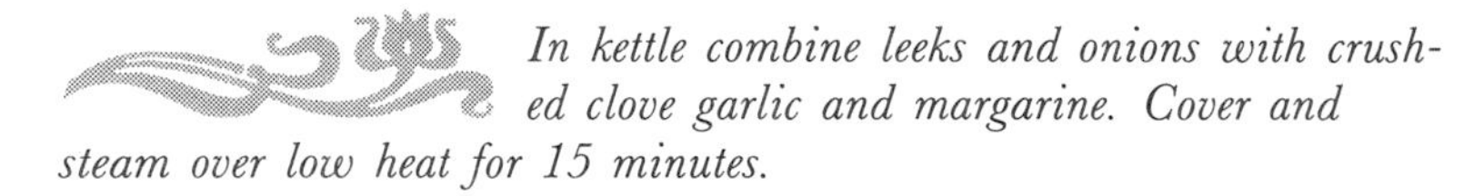

In kettle combine leeks and onions with crushed clove garlic and margarine. Cover and steam over low heat for 15 minutes.

Add potatoes and 4 cups of chicken stock or broth, and simmer for 15 minutes.

Coarsely chop watercress, discarding stems. Add all but ½ cup to the soup. Simmer, covered, for 20 minutes.

Purée soup through medium disk of food mill or use blender or food processor. Return to kettle.

Add last 2 cups of chicken stock, milk, heavy cream and the reserved watercress.

Simmer the soup until heated through. Season with salt and pepper to taste. Ladle into bowls.

TUSCAN WHITE BEAN AND TOMATO SOUP

For a perfect summer supper, serve this hearty country soup with crusty bread and a tossed green salad.

1-pound Great Northern beans
4 cups chicken stock, preferably homemade
2 bay leaves
⅓ cup olive oil
¾-pound onions, thinly sliced
4 medium celery stalks, thinly sliced
3 medium carrots, thinly sliced
½ cup pancetta
10-ounces smoked ham, coarsely diced
2 teaspoons sugar
4 cloves garlic, minced
5-pounds, (about 12) large, ripe tomatoes, peeled, seeded and chopped
¼ cup fresh lemon juice
Salt and freshly ground pepper
Minced fresh parsley

Makes 4 quarts.

Soak beans overnight in enough cold water to cover in stockpot or boil beans 3 minutes, then soak 1 hour.

Add stock and bay leaves to beans. Simmer until tender, about 1 hour. Heat oil in large heavy saucepan over medium-high heat. Add onions, celery and carrots and stir until softened and just beginning to color or about 5 minutes. Add pancetta and stir until translucent or about 3 minutes. Add ham, sugar and garlic and stir 5 minutes. Stir in tomatoes and bring to boil. Reduce heat to simmer. Add beans and liquid and cook until thick, stirring occasionally, about 45 minutes. Blend in lemon juice. Season with salt and pepper. Let soup stand at room temperature several hours. Garnish with parsley before serving.

GARDEN GOURMET TOMATO SOUP

The perfect beginning for an elegant black tie dinner.

8 to 10 tomatoes, peeled and seeded
½ teaspoon sugar
½ teaspoon salt
½ teaspoon black pepper
1 large clove garlic, peeled and minced
3 tablespoons butter
1 cup fresh mushrooms, finely sliced
1 pinch thyme
¼ cup fresh basil, chopped
3 strips cooked bacon, crumbled
1 tablespoon gin
½ cup or more whipping cream
Green onions, optional garnish

Serves 4 to 6.

Purée tomatoes in blender or food processor. Add sugar, salt, pepper and one half of the garlic to tomatoes and blend well.

Melt butter in fry pan over medium-high heat, and add mushrooms, remaining garlic, thyme and basil. Cook until mushrooms are just done and add bacon. Add gin to mushrooms and ignite. Reduce to low heat; add tomato mixture and blend well.

Pour in cream and simmer 20 minutes (add more cream if soup is too thick).

Garnish each bowl if you like with unsweetened whipped cream and thinly sliced green onions.

ITALIAN TOMATO AND BASIL SOUP

Serve hot or cold, as a first course or for lunch with a sandwich.

2-pounds ripe pear-shaped tomatoes
2 tablespoons olive oil
½ cup fresh basil leaves
½ cup chicken broth
½ cup whipping cream
Salt
Pepper

Serves 6.

Cut tomatoes into chunks. Put oil, tomatoes and ¼ cup basil into a 3 to 4 quart pan. Cook, stirring, over medium-high heat until tomatoes mash easily; 10 to 15 minutes. Pour into a blender; add broth and cream. Whirl until smooth. Season to taste with salt and pepper. Serve hot or cold.

ITALIAN SOUP

Complete this quick mid-week zesty meal with a crusty French or sourdough bread and a crisp, tossed green salad.

1½ pounds Italian sausage
2 cloves garlic, crushed
1 mcdium onion, chopped
1 28-ounce can tomatoes
3 cans beef consomme (not bouillon)
1½ cups dry red wine
½ teaspoon basil
3 teaspoons parsley
2 zucchini, sliced
3 cups bow tie noodles
Parmesan cheese, grated

Serves 6 to 8.

If the sausage has a casing on it, be sure to remove it. Mix the sausage, garlic and onion together and brown until meat is done. Drain.

Add tomatoes, consomme and wine. Add the spices and zucchini. Simmer for 30 minutes.

Add the bow tie noodles and cook until the noodles are done.

Pour the hot soup into bowls and sprinkle with Parmesan cheese.

PARTY ONION SOUP

Can be made ahead. A great soup for after skiing.

Soup:
10 large onions
½ cup butter
¼ cup flour
4 quarts meat broth, canned regular-strength or homemade
1 cup dry white wine or ¼ cup lemon juice with ¾ cup water
Salt
Pepper

Condiments:
2 cups Swiss cheese, shredded
3 to 4 cups croutons
1½ to 2 cups tomatoes, seeded and diced
1 cup green onions, sliced
½ pound crisp cooked bacon, crumbled

Serves 16.

Cut the onions in half vertically, then in thin vertical slices. Melt the butter in a 6 to 8-quart Dutch oven. Add onions, cover and cook until limp, or about 10 minutes. Uncover and cook, stirring often, until onions are light brown, about 20 to 25 minutes. If necessary, reduce heat. Sprinkle flour over onions. Cook, stirring for about 1 minute. Remove from heat and gradually stir in 2 quarts of broth. Return to heat, add wine, and bring to boil while stirring. Cover and reduce heat to keep broth simmering for 30 to 40 minutes. If making ahead, cover and refrigerate. Before serving, add remaining 2 quarts broth and reheat slowly until piping hot. Season to taste with salt and pepper. Serve with condiments.

CREAM OF CHICKEN, ASPARAGUS AND WILD RICE SOUP

½ cup wild rice
6½ cups chicken broth
¼ cup butter
3 large cloves garlic, minced
1 medium onion, chopped
2 carrots, finely diced
1-pound trimmed asparagus, finely diced
½ cup all-purpose flour
½ cup extra dry vermouth
½ teaspoon thyme
1 bay leaf
¼ teaspoon nutmeg
Salt and pepper to taste
4 cups half-and-half
Parsley, minced (optional)
Chives, minced (optional)

Serves 8.

Soak wild rice in hot water 30 minutes. Drain. In a saucepan combine wild rice and 2 cups chicken broth. Bring to a slow boil and reduce heat to a simmer. Cook for 45 minutes, covered. When done, turn off heat and allow rice to sit, covered, for an additional 15 minutes. Set aside and let cool. The rice can be prepared the day before and kept in the refrigerator.

In a Dutch oven, melt the butter and sauté the garlic and onion until tender. Add the carrots and asparagus and cook until tender. Mix in the flour and cook over low heat for approximately 10 minutes, stirring frequently. Pour in the remaining chicken broth and vermouth. Using a wire whisk, blend until smooth. Add the seasonings. Slowly add the half-and-half. Simmer for 20 minutes. Fold in the prepared wild rice and serve. You may want to garnish with chopped chives or parsley.

Note: If asparagus isn't available, other vegetables may be substituted (broccoli, cauliflower, green beans or zucchini are suggested).

AVGOLEMONO SOUP

A traditional Greek soup. Seattle celebrates its Greek community with an annual festival.

6 cups strong chicken broth
½ cup long grain rice
Salt
1 egg
2 egg yolks
¼ cup lemon juice
Pepper

Serves 6.

Bring chicken broth to boil in soup pot. Add rice, salt to taste, and cook until rice is soft; about 20 minutes. In a separate bowl, beat egg and egg yolks well. Add lemon juice beating together thoroughly with rotary beater. Dilute mixture with a little of the hot broth, beating continuously. Add egg mixture to soup, stir well, bring to boil. Remove from heat and let stand 5 minutes before serving. Add pepper to taste.

COLD SOUR CHERRY SOUP

Reflecting the traditional Scandanavian fishing villages of the Northwest.

3 cups plus 2 tablespoons cold water
1 cup sugar
1 cinnamon stick
4 cups pitted sour cherries or drained canned sour cherries
1 tablespoon arrowroot or cornstarch
¼ cup heavy cream
¾ cup dry red wine, chilled

Serves 6.

In a 2-quart saucepan, combine 3 cups water, sugar and cinnamon stick. Bring to a boil and add cherries. Partially cover and simmer over low heat for 35 to 40 minutes if cherries are fresh, or 10 minutes if they are canned. Remove cinnamon stick.

Mix arrowroot or cornstarch and 2 tablespoons cold water into a paste, then beat into the cherry soup. Stirring constantly, bring the soup almost to a boil. Reduce the heat and simmer about 2 minutes or until clear and slightly thickened. Pour into a shallow glass or stainless steel bowl and refrigerate until chilled. Before serving stir in the cream and wine. Serve in bowls that have been pre-chilled.

GREAT GAZPACHO

Versatile! Serve cold as a soup, a salsa for Mexican food, a pre-dinner appetizer, or as a sauce over eggs, pasta and meats.

4 cups cold tomato juice
1 large onion, chopped
2 cups fresh tomatoes, finely diced
1 cup fresh green pepper, finely diced
1 large cucumber, seeded and finely diced
2 green onions, finely chopped
1 clove garlic, pressed
1 teaspoon honey
2 tablespoons red wine vinegar
¼ cup fresh parsley, chopped
Juice of ½ lemon
Juice of 1 whole lime
2 tablespoons olive oil
Dash of tabasco
1 teaspoon salt
1 teaspoon black pepper
1 teaspoon tarragon
1 teaspoon basil
1 teaspoon cumin
1 cup celery, finely diced, optional
½ teaspoon Worcestershire sauce, optional

Serves 4 to 6.

Chopping and dicing may be done by hand for uniformity or in a food processor. The food processor will save time, but the pieces won't all be the same size.

Combine all ingredients and refrigerate. Covered tightly, it will keep for one week.

NORTHWEST-STYLE CRAB SOUP

Serve this company-quality soup with a Washington State Riesling.

½ cup butter
¼ cup all-purpose flour
4 cups milk
2 tablespoons onion, chopped
2 teaspoons instant chicken bouillon powder
2 teaspoons fresh parsley, minced
1 teaspoon salt
½ teaspoon pepper, freshly ground
½ teaspoon nutmeg, freshly grated
½-pound crabmeat, Dungeness preferred
½-pound fresh asparagus, trimmed, peeled and cut into 1-inch lengths

Makes 8 cups.

Melt butter in large, heavy saucepan over medium-low heat. Whisk in flour and cook 3 minutes. Gradually whisk in milk. Add onion, bouillon, parsley, salt, pepper and nutmeg. Increase heat and bring to boil. Reduce heat and simmer until soup begins to thicken, stirring occasionally; about 10 minutes. Add crabmeat and cook until soup is creamy, 10 to 15 minutes. Add asparagus and cook until crisp-tender, 5 to 7 minutes. Adjust seasoning. Serve immediately.

FULL-OF-SEAFOOD CHOWDER

3 cups potatoes, cubed
¼ cup butter
½ cup onion, chopped
½ cup celery, chopped
2 cloves garlic, minced
1 10-ounce jar small oysters, drained with liquid reserved
1 6½-ounce can minced clams, drained with liquid reserved
1 6½-ounce can tiny shrimp, drained with liquid reserved
⅓ cup dry white wine
1 teaspoon chicken-seasoned stock base, optional
1 teaspoon salt
½ teaspoon thyme leaves, crushed
½ teaspoon nutmeg
½ teaspoon pepper
1 bay leaf
5 tablespoons flour
⅓ cup cold water
1-pound cod fillets, cubed
½ cup green pepper, diced
½ pint whipping cream
¼ cup parsley, chopped
1 2-ounce jar pimiento, chopped

Serves 6 to 8.

Cook potatoes in boiling salted water until tender, but not overcooked. Drain and set aside. In a large soup kettle or saucepan, melt butter and saute onion, celery and garlic for 5 minutes.

Drain oysters, clams and shrimp, saving liquids in a 4-cup measuring cup. Add enough water to the liquids to measure 3 cups. Pour liquids into saucepan with onion mixture.

Add wine, chicken-seasoned stock base, salt, thyme, nutmeg, pepper and bay leaf. Cover and simmer 15 minutes.

Mix flour and cold water to a smooth paste. Add to liquid, stirring constantly. Cook until thickened.

Add cod, green pepper and oysters. Simmer, uncovered, for 10 to 15 minutes. Remove bay leaf. Add potatoes, whipping cream, clams, shrimp, parsley and pimiento. Heat through until simmering.

Serve hot with crusty French bread and a glass of white wine.

NORTHWEST SALMON CHOWDER

Pair this classic favorite with a well-chilled Chardonnay. Serve with Yakima Apple and Pear Salad.

½ cup celery, chopped
½ cup onion, chopped
½ cup green pepper, chopped
1 clove garlic, minced
3 tablespoons butter or margarine
1 cup white potatoes, diced
1 cup carrot, shredded
2 cups chicken broth
1½ teaspoons salt
½ teaspoon pepper
¼ teaspoon dill weed
1 17-ounce can cream-style corn
1 13-ounce can evaporated milk or 2 cups half-and-half
2 cups salmon, cooked and flaked

Serves 4 to 6.

In a 3-quart saucepan, sauté celery, onion, pepper and garlic in butter or margarine until onion is translucent. Add potatoes, carrots, chicken broth and seasonings. Simmer for 40 minutes.

Add corn, evaporated milk or half-and-half and salmon. Heat thoroughly, about 30 minutes, and serve.

HEARTY CRAB CHOWDER

An excellent choice for aprés ski dining! Serve with a generous supply of garlic bread.

4 slices bacon, chopped
1 cup onions, diced
6 medium new potatoes, cubed and unpeeled
½ cup green pepper, diced
1 cup celery, diced
1 cup carrots, peeled and diced
1 clove garlic, minced
2 cups clam juice
1 cup dry white wine
1 teaspoon salt
½ teaspoon lemon pepper
1 teaspoon Worcestershire sauce
4 drops tabasco sauce
2 cups flaked crab meat (Dungeness)
2 cups half-and-half

Serves 6 to 8.

Sauté the bacon in a 3 or 4 quart kettle until browned.

Stir in onion, potatoes, green pepper, celery, carrot and garlic and heat 2 minutes.

Pour in the clam juice and wine, stirring well. Add the salt, lemon pepper, Worcestershire sauce and tabasco sauce. Bring to a boil; cover kettle and lower heat. Simmer 15 minutes or until potatoes are tender. Add crab meat and half-and-half. Heat until hot, but not boiling.

NORTHWEST BOUILLABAISSE

A dish created to celebrate the Northwest's finest seafood.

8 tablespoons olive oil
1 cup onion, coarsely chopped
½ cup leeks, white bottoms only, coarsely chopped
2 teaspoons garlic, minced
¾ cup carrots, coarsely chopped
1 teaspoon fennel seed
3-pounds halibut or cod fish trimmings, gills removed
1 bay leaf
1 teaspoon thyme
3 tablespoons parsley, chopped
1 2-inch strip of orange peel
2 cups dry white wine
1 to 2 teaspoons red pepper, crushed
Salt to taste
Pepper to taste
2 cups fresh tomatoes, peeled and chopped
1 teaspoon saffron threads
2 Dungeness crabs, cracked and cleaned
2-pounds white fish, cut into uniform chunks
1-pound scallops
2-pounds prawns, cleaned and deveined
24 mussels in the shell, optional
24 steamer clams in the shell, optional

Serves 10.

Prepare a court bouillon by heating 4 tablespoons olive oil in a large pot. Sauté the onions, leeks and garlic over a medium-low heat, stirring occasionally, until the onions are translucent but not brown. Add carrots and fennel and sauté briefly. Add fish trimmings, herbs, orange peel, white wine, red pepper, salt, pepper, remaining olive oil and sufficient water to cover. Bring to a boil and continue boiling vigorously for 20 minutes. Strain the broth, pressing down on the solids. Skim and return the broth to the pot. Add tomatoes and saffron. Bring court bouillon to a boil, add crab and simmer covered for 8 minutes. Add fish, scallops and prawns and bring to a boil. If you include mussels or clams, scrub carefully, and cook separately in just enough water to cover the bottom of a saucepan. Cook until they open; remove from water and keep warm. Add to boiling seafood, simmer 3 minutes and serve.

POZOLE

A meal in itself. Rich in the Yakima Valley's Mexican heritage.

**2 large fresh pork hocks,
split in 2 or 3 pieces each
2 quarts water
1 16-ounce can whole tomatoes
2 16-ounce cans hominy, drained
2 medium onions, finely chopped
4 teaspoons salt**

**Fresh Toppings, as desired:
Shredded lettuce
Chopped radishes
Thinly sliced green onions
Shredded carrots
Chopped avocado
Cream cheese, cubed, or other soft cheese
(such as Jack cheese), shredded
2 limes, cut in wedges
Liquid hot-pepper seasoning (optional)
Chopped chiles or horseradish (optional)**

Serves 8 to 10.

Put pork hocks into a large kettle with water, tomatoes, hominy, onions and salt. Simmer for 2 to 3 hours or until the meat begins to separate from bones. Remove pork hocks from soup. Cool both meat and soup. When the soup is cold, skim off the fat. Remove meat from hocks, discarding fat and bones. Cut the meat into small pieces. Just before serving, add the meat to soup and reheat, adding additional salt if needed.

Serve with an assortment of chopped fresh vegetables, cheese and lime wedges to be added to individual servings. For spicier soup, serve with hot-pepper seasoning, chiles or horseradish.

FISH AND SEAFOOD

FISH AND SEAFOOD

HALIBUT OSCAR

Halibut:
2¼-pounds halibut fillets, cut into 6 equal pieces
1 tablespoon pickling spices
1 small onion, coarsely chopped
1 cup dry white wine
18 asparagus spears, cooked until tender-crisp
12 Dungeness crab legs or large chunks of crab meat

Oscar Sauce:
3 egg yolks
3 tablespoons tarragon wine vinegar
1 teaspoon shallots, chopped
15 whole peppercorns, crushed
1 tablespoon water
1¼ cups butter, melted and skimmed
¾ teaspoon dried tarragon, crushed
Juice of ½ lemon
Salt
Cayenne pepper

Serves 6.

To prepare halibut, rinse the halibut pieces. Bring 1½ quarts salted water, pickling spices, onion and dry white wine to a boil in a large skillet. Lower heat, cover and simmer 20 minutes. Add the halibut fillets and poach just until done, allowing 10 minutes per inch of thickness.

Place the fish on a warm serving platter, removing any skin from the fish. Top each fish piece with 3 asparagus spears and 2 crab legs or large chunks of crab meat. Cover with foil and place in a warm oven while preparing Oscar sauce.

To prepare sauce, put the egg yolks in the top part of a double boiler; add water to the bottom part and let it simmer.

In another saucepan, put the tarragon vinegar, shallots and crushed peppercorns. Boil until most of the vinegar is cooked away. Set aside to cool. Add 1 tablespoon water and strain into the egg yolks.

Beat the egg yolk mixture well and place over simmering water, beating constantly with a wire whisk, until the mixture looks foamy and just barely thick. Do not overcook the egg yolks. It is best to take the top part of the double boiler off the water toward the end of the beating to make sure the egg yolks do not overcook. Stir in butter, tarragon, lemon juice, salt and cayenne pepper.

Serve sauce with fish as a wonderful complement.

HEAVENLY HALIBUT

2-pounds skinless halibut or other fish fillets, fresh or frozen
2 tablespoons lemon juice
½ cup Parmesan cheese, freshly grated
¼ cup butter or margarine, softened
3 tablespoons mayonnaise
3 tablespoons green onions, chopped
¼ teaspoon salt
Dash of tabasco sauce

Serves 6.

Thaw fillets if frozen. Pat dry with paper towels. Place fillets in single layer on well-greased bake-and-serve platter.

Combine remaining ingredients in a small bowl; set aside. Broil fillets about 4-inches from heat for 6 to 8 minutes or until fillets flake easily. Remove from heat and spread with cheese mixture. Return to oven and broil 2 to 3 minutes or until lightly browned.

LEMON-RICE STUFFED SALMON

Undeniably, Northwest waters are home to premium fish. Here is a deceptively simple way of preparing a Northwest specialty that results in pure elegance.

1 4-pound, whole salmon
2½ tablespoons butter
½ cup celery, finely chopped
¾ cup fresh mushrooms, sliced
1 cup cooked rice
½ cup green onions, chopped
2 to 3 tablespoons pimento, diced
2 tablespoons lemon juice
¾ teaspoon salt
⅛ teaspoon dried thyme, crushed
Lemon pepper to taste
Oil
Lemon slices
Parsley

Serves 8.

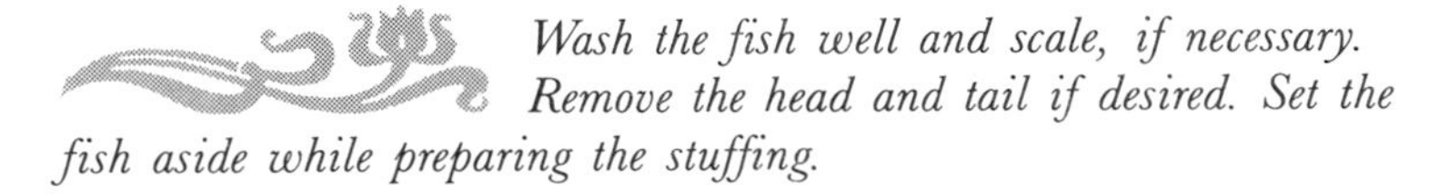

Wash the fish well and scale, if necessary. Remove the head and tail if desired. Set the fish aside while preparing the stuffing.

Heat the butter in a skillet. Add the celery and mushrooms and sauté about 5 minutes.

Combine the cooked rice, green onions, pimento, lemon juice, salt, thyme and lemon pepper in a bowl; add the celery-mushroom mixture and blend well.

Preheat oven to 450°.

Pat the fish dry and fill the cavity with stuffing. Close opening with small skewers or toothpicks. Measure fish at the thickest part, including the stuffing.

Brush fish with oil. Place in a greased, shallow baking pan. Bake 10 minutes per inch of thickness. Remove skewers and upper skin if desired. Garnish with lemon slices and parsley.

COLD POACHED SALMON WITH HERB MAYONNAISE

This poached salmon is not masked by the sauce, but instead, is complemented by delicate seasonings. An entree versatile enough for the most formal of buffets or an outdoor excursion.

Poached Salmon:
2 slices onion
1 stalk celery
2 slices lemon
4 peppercorns
2 cups clam juice
½ cup dry white wine
4 fresh salmon steaks or fillets

Herb Mayonnaise:
1 cup mayonnaise
1 tablespoon lemon juice
Dash of Worcestershire sauce
½ teaspoon sugar
¼ teaspoon white pepper
1 tablespoon dill weed
2 tablespoons parsley, chopped
2 green onions, finely chopped

Serves 4.

To prepare poached salmon, combine all ingredients except salmon in large skillet. Bring to a boil over medium-high heat. Reduce heat to low. Add salmon and poach gently until opaque, about 10 minutes. Carefully remove salmon from liquid and chill. Serve with herb mayonnaise.

To prepare herb mayonnaise, blend all ingredients. Chill. Makes 1 cup.

SAUCE FOR SALMON

This sauce captures the intrinsic goodness of fish by balancing the fish's moisture content, allowing for exceptional flavor and tenderness. Also experiment, using on vegetables and potatoes.

¼-pound melted butter
4 tablespoons ketchup
5 tablespoons soy sauce
3 tablespoons Worcestershire
1½ tablespoons prepared mustard
1 clove garlic, pressed

Enough for 8 salmon steaks.

Combine ingredients and cover salmon or other fish during barbeque.

STUFFED SOLE

2 tablespoons butter
½ cup green onion, finely chopped
¼ cup celery, chopped
½ cup mushrooms, chopped
1½ to 2-pounds sole fillets
2 to 4 tablespoons butter, melted
½ teaspoon salt
⅛ teaspoon pepper
½ teaspoon poultry seasoning
½ cup dry bread crumbs
½ cup tiny shrimp
Cheese sauce, optional

Serves 4 to 6.

In a skillet, melt 2 tablespoons butter. Sauté onion, celery and mushrooms. Set aside. Cut fillets in half, if necessary, so each is about 2-inches wide. Brush fillets skin side up with melted butter. Combine salt, pepper and poultry seasoning. Sprinkle fillets with bread crumbs and seasoning mixture.

Place spoonful of sautéed onion mix on each fillet, then a few shrimp. Roll fillet gently and place seam side down on baking dish. Top with cheese sauce, if desired. Cover dish with waxed paper. Bake at 350° for 25 minutes or cook in the microwave on high for 8 to 10 minutes, rotating dish once halfway through cooking. Let stand 5 minutes before serving.

SOLE AND SHRIMP

This can be prepared ahead of time.

1-pound sole fillets
¼-pound small cooked shrimp
3 tablespoons fine bread crumbs
¼ teaspoon pepper
2 tablespoons lemon juice
2 tablespoons light mayonnaise
2 tablespoons green onions, thinly sliced
1 small clove garlic, pressed
1½ tablespoons butter, softened

Serves 4.

Butter a shallow baking dish. Place one half of the fillets in an even layer on the bottom of the dish. Sprinkle with one half of the shrimp, bread crumbs, pepper and lemon juice. Repeat the layers.

Mix together mayonnaise, green onion and garlic. Spread over dish and dot with butter on the top.

Cover and chill if made ahead. Bake at 350°, covered, until the fish is opaque in the center, about 30 minutes. Bake 40 minutes if fish is chilled.

TURBAN OF SOLE WITH SALMON MOUSSE

Salmon Filling:
2-pounds fresh salmon, boned and skinned
¾ cup heavy cream
1 teaspoon kosher salt
Pinch of nutmeg

8 fillets of sole, approximately 6-ounces each

Grated Cucumber:
2 cups cucumber, peeled and grated
Salt
3 tablespoons butter

Basic Bechamel Sauce:
4 tablespoons butter
3 tablespoons flour
2 cups fish stock
¼ cup Pernod

Sauce Nantua:
1 cup heavy cream
1 teaspoon cornstarch
1 teaspoon tomato paste
12 prawns in shell

Serves 8.

To make salmon filling, put salmon, cream, salt and nutmeg in food processor and process until smooth.

Lay fillet of sole flat on counter, skin side up. Place 3-ounces of salmon mousse in center and roll fillet over filling to form a cylinder. Secure with a toothpick. Place rolls upright in a buttered baking dish. Mousse should be even with top of fillet. Place buttered wax paper over top of baking dish and tie with string to secure. Bake at 400° for 20 minutes.

To make grated cucumbers, salt the cucumber and let stand for 30 minutes. Rinse and drain well. Sauté in butter. Keep warm over low heat.

To make Bechamel sauce, combine ingredients.

To make sauce Nantua, add 1 cup of cream mixed with cornstarch and tomato paste to the Bechamel sauce. Add the prawns and let simmer gently for 20 minutes. Let cook slighly and pureé in blender. Strain and season to taste.

Place baked sole turban on bed of ¼ cup sautéed cucumbers to serve. Top with sauce Nantua.

TROUT WITH SHRIMP AND CHIVE SAUCE

This extremely simple dish is no more difficult to prepare than pan-fried trout, but much more divine.

Trout:
4 12-ounce trout, boned
Salt, to taste
Freshly ground pepper, to taste
⅓ cup flour
2 tablespoons butter
2 tablespoons oil

Shrimp And Chive Sauce:
2 tablespoons butter
¼ cup onion, minced
¼ cup dry white wine
1 tablespoon white wine vinegar
1 cup heavy cream
Salt, to taste
Pepper, to taste
¼-pound tiny cooked shrimp
3 tablespoons fresh chives, chopped

Serves 4.

Rinse the fish and pat dry. Sprinkle inside and out with the salt and pepper. Dredge lightly in flour, shaking off the excess. Melt the butter and oil in a large skillet. Sauté the fish for 4 to 5 minutes on each side, or until done. If skin starts to brown too quickly, reduce the heat. Transfer to a heated platter and cover with foil.

To prepare sauce, scrape up any brown bits from the bottom of the skillet. Discard together with the cooking oil. Wipe out the skillet with a paper towel. Add the butter and melt over a low heat. Sauté the onions until soft, about 5 minutes. Add the wine and vinegar. Increase the heat and boil until reduced to 1 tablespoon. Stir in the cream. Season with salt and pepper. Reduce until the sauce thickens and coats the back of a wooden spoon. Stir in the shrimp. Simmer over low heat until heated through. Remove from heat and stir in chives.

Discard the skin from the top of the trout. Transfer to a serving platter. Spoon the sauce over the top of each trout. Serve immediately.

IMPERIAL TROUT AND PASTA

3-pounds trout
1 tablespoon butter
⅓ cup milk
⅓ cup water
Salt and freshly ground black pepper to taste
3 bay leaves
4 cups angel hair pasta, cooked and tossed with butter and pepper

Sauce:
½ cup butter
¾-pound mushrooms, sliced
2 cloves garlic, pressed
4 green onions including tops, finely chopped
¼-pound shrimp, cooked
¼-pound lobster, cooked
2 tablespoons all-purpose flour
1 cup milk
1 cup heavy cream
Salt and freshly ground black pepper to taste

Freshly grated Parmesan cheese
Paprika
Sprigs of parsley
Fresh lemon juice
Lemon slices

Serves 4.

Skin and bone trout and place side-by-side in non-stick skillet with 1 tablespoon of butter. Add just enough milk and water to come halfway up fish. Sprinkle with salt and pepper and add bay leaves. Cover pan and heat liquid to boiling. Reduce heat and cook for 15 minutes or until fish flakes easily, but is still firm. Remove fish from skillet with pancake spatula and place on bed of hot angel hair pasta. Discard bay leaves. Reduce remaining poaching liquid to ½ cup and set aside.

In medium skillet, melt ½ cup butter and sauté mushrooms and garlic for 5 minutes, stirring occasionally. Add green onions and cook for additional 5 minutes. Add shrimp and lobster; heat thoroughly. Stirring constantly, sprinkle with flour and cook for 2 minutes. Gradually add milk, cream and reduced poaching liquid and simmer for 10 minutes over low heat until smooth and thickened. Season with salt and pepper.

Reheat fish in microwave for 1½ minutes. Pour sauce around edge of fish and sprinkle liberally with Parmesan cheese and paprika. Add sprigs of parsley and squeeze lemon juice over top. Serve with lemon slices, additional Parmesan cheese and freshly ground black pepper.

SCALLOP KABOBS

1-pound scallops
4-ounces button mushrooms
2 tablespoons vegetable oil
2 tablespoons soy sauce
2 tablespoons lemon juice
2 tablespoons snipped parsley
½ teaspoon salt
Dash of pepper
12 bacon slices
Green pepper chunks
Cherry tomatoes
1 13½-ounce can pineapple chunks or fresh pineapple chunks
Melted butter

Serves 4 to 6.

If large sea scallops are used, cut into 3 or 4 pieces. Wash scallops. Remove any shell particles.

Place scallops and mushrooms in a shallow glass dish. Combine oil, soy sauce, lemon juice, parsley, salt and pepper. Pour over scallops and mushrooms. Cover and refrigerate for 30 minutes, turning once.

Partially fry bacon. Drain and cut slices in half. On skewers alternate scallops, bacon, green pepper, mushrooms, tomatoes and pineapple.

Broil kabobs 3-inches from heat for 5 to 8 minutes, turning once and basting with butter.

SCALLOPS AND RED PEPPER PASTA

1 lemon
12 to 16-ounces spaghetti
Water
¼ cup butter or margarine
¼ cup olive oil
1 to 2 medium to large red bell peppers, cored, seeded and cut into thin slices
2 cloves garlic, minced or pressed
¼ to ½ teaspoon dried hot red pepper, crushed
1-pound large scallops, cut into ¼-inch slices, or ¾-pound tiny bay scallops plus ¼-pound large, peeled shrimp
¾ cup chicken broth, regular strength
¾ cup parsley, finely chopped
Salt and pepper
8 tablespoons Parmesan cheese, fresh grated

Serves 4.

With a zester, cut peel from lemon in fine shreds, or thinly pare yellow layer of skin and cut into fine slivers. Reserve lemon zest and juice. Cook spaghetti in 4 quarts of boiling water until tender to bite (al dente) about 9 minutes. Drain, rinse with cold water and let stand to drain again. Heat butter and olive oil in a 10 to 12-inch frying pan over medium-high heat. Add bell pepper slivers, garlic and crushed pepper. Cook, stirring about 1 minute. Lift out bell peppers with a slotted spoon. Add scallops or shrimp, lemon zest and lemon juice. Stir for 2 minutes. Add chicken broth, cover pan and lower heat for about 3 to 5 minutes.

Toss pasta with hot scallops in broth, bell peppers and parsley. Add salt and pepper to taste. Keep over very low heat until hot, then serve immediately, topping each serving with about 2 tablespoons Parmesan cheese.

GREEN SHRIMP

Shrimp:
¼ cup salt
1 bay leaf
1 teaspoon caraway seed
½ teaspoon dry mustard
½ teaspoon pepper
5-pounds raw shrimp in shell

Sauce:
¼-pound butter or margarine
2 teaspoons soy sauce
1 teaspoon tabasco sauce
1 teaspoon salt
1 tablespoon Worcestershire sauce
Juice of 2 large fresh lemons

Serves 4 to 6.

To cook shrimp, bring 3 to 4 quarts water to boil. Add salt, bay leaf, caraway, mustard and pepper. Add shrimp and cook 20 minutes. Drain and serve.

To prepare sauce, (while shrimp cooks) melt butter over low heat and add seasonings. Keep warm.

To serve, give each person a small dish of sauce to accompany shrimp. Serve with French bread and tossed green salad.

CAJUN PRAWNS DIANE

This dish is best if made only two servings at a time. If you want to make more, do so in separate batches but serve while piping hot.

1¾-pounds medium-size shrimp
¾ cup butter
¼ cup green onions, very finely chopped
¼ teaspoon salt
½ teaspoon garlic, minced
½ teaspoon cayenne pepper, ground
¼ teaspoon white pepper
¼ teaspoon black pepper
¼ teaspoon dried sweet basil leaves
¼ teaspoon dried thyme leaves
⅛ teaspoon dried oregano leaves
½-pound mushrooms, cut into ¼-inch thick slices
6 tablespoons fish stock or water
3 tablespoons fresh parsley, very finely chopped

Serves 2.

Have the shrimp rinsed, peeled and ready for use. In large skillet melt 1 stick butter over high heat. When almost melted, add the green onions, salt, garlic, the ground peppers, basil, thyme and oregano; stir well. Add the shrimp and sauté just until they turn pink, about 1 minute, shaking the pan (rather than stirring) in a back-and-forth motion. Add the mushrooms and ¼ cup of the stock or water. Then add the remaining 4 tablespoons of butter in chunks and continue cooking, continuing to shake the pan. Before the butter chunks are completely melted, add the parsley, then the remaining 2 tablespoons stock or water, continue cooking and shaking the pan until all ingredients are mixed thoroughly and butter sauce is consistency of cream. Serve immediately in a bowl with lots of french bread on the side, or serve over pasta or rice.

BARBEQUED CRAB

1 large onion, thinly sliced
3 cloves garlic, minced
4 celery stalks, chopped
4 tablespoons butter
1 tablespoon parsley, minced
4 peppercorns, crushed
1 bay leaf
2 tablespoons Worcestershire sauce
½ teaspoon tabasco sauce
2 10-ounce cans beef consomme
1 cup tomato juice
4 tablespoons soy sauce
2 large crabs, cracked and cut up

Serves 4 to 6.

Sauté onion, garlic and celery in butter. Add parsley, peppercorns, bay leaf, Worcestershire sauce, tabasco sauce, beef consomme and tomato juice. Cover and simmer for 30 minutes. Add soy sauce.

Pour sauce over cracked crab in a pan. Bake at 350° for 20 to 30 minutes. Serve hot in bowls, ladling the broth over each serving.

NORTHWEST CRABBY CHEESE SANDWICH

½ cup mayonnaise
½ cup chili sauce
1 cup Dungeness crab
4 cups medium cheddar cheese, grated
¼ cup green olives, chopped, optional
¼ cup green onions, chopped
¼ cup parsley, chopped
¼ cup green bell peppers, chopped
¼ cup celery, chopped
12 slices sourdough bread
½ cup butter, melted

Makes 6 sandwiches.

In a medium bowl stir together the mayonnaise, chili sauce, and crab.

Add the cheese, green olives, green onions, parsley, green peppers, and celery. Mix thoroughly.

Divide the filling among six slices of bread and top with the remaining slices of bread.

Brush outsides of sandwiches with butter and grill in a large frypan, medium heat, or under the broiler until cheese melts and bread is golden brown.

WILD RICE AND SHRIMP CASSEROLE

1 cup uncooked wild rice
1 cup uncooked white rice
1-pound mushrooms
2 tablespoons butter or margarine
2 medium onions, chopped
1 green pepper, chopped
2 cups celery, diced
1-pound shrimp
½-pound toasted almonds
2 10-ounce cans mushroom soup
Grated Cheddar cheese

Serves 8 to 10.

According to package directions, cook white and wild rice separately. Sauté mushrooms in butter, remove. Sauté onions and green pepper. Combine the rice, celery, onions, peppers, mushrooms, shrimp, almonds, and soup. Place in a greased 9 by 12-inch casserole, cover with cheese, and bake 1 hour at 325°.

Note: Crab or chicken may be substituted for the shrimp. Sliced water chestnuts may be substituted for the almonds.

SEAFOOD CHOW MEIN

7-ounces pan-fried noodles
½-pound prawns, shelled, deveined and rinsed
¼-pound scallops
¼ teaspoon salt
1 teaspoon wine
½ egg white
1 tablespoon cornstarch
3 tablespoons oil
1 clove garlic, minced
1 small onion, wedged
¼-pound pea pods
1 cup bok choy leaves
¼ cup water chestnuts, sliced
⅓ cup bamboo shoots, sliced
2 large forest mushrooms, soaked, rinsed and sliced ¼-inch thick
¾ cup soup stock
1 tablespoon oyster sauce
½ teaspoon salt or salt to taste
Cornstarch and water for thickening

Serves 4.

Prepare pan-fried noodles according to instructions. Place on large platter.

Cut prawns in half lengthwise. Slice scallops into ¼-inch thick slices. Combine with salt, wine, egg white and cornstarch. Set aside.

Heat wok and add 2 tablespoons of oil and garlic. Stir-fry prawns and scallops for 2 minutes or until done. Remove from wok and set aside. Add 1 tablespoon oil to wok and add all vegetables. Stir-fry a few seconds. Add soup stock, oyster sauce and salt. Cover, bring to a boil and cook 30 seconds. Add seafood to vegetables, thicken with cornstarch mixture and gently stir to combine. Pour ingredients over pan-fried noodles and serve.

SEAFOOD PIE

¼-pound Swiss cheese, grated
¼-pound Cheddar cheese, grated
1 pie crust, baked in 10-inch springform pan
1-pound cooked crabmeat
1 cup dry-roasted cashews
3 cups whipping cream
8 eggs, beaten to blend
Salt and freshly ground pepper
2 tablespoons butter
¼ teaspoon dried tarragon, crumbled
¼ teaspoon freshly grated nutmeg
1 large red onion, minced
1½-pounds frozen chopped spinach, thawed, drained and squeezed dry

Serves 10 to 12.

Position rack in center of oven and preheat to 450°. Sprinkle cheeses over baked pie crust. Cover with crabmeat. Top with cashews. Mix cream and eggs. Season generously with salt and pepper. Pour half of egg mixture into crust; set remaining mixture aside. Place pie in oven. Reduce temperature to 350°. Bake pie until custard is set but not browned, 35 to 40 minutes.

Meanwhile, melt butter in heavy, large skillet over medium-low heat. Stir in tarragon, nutmeg and ⅛ teaspoon pepper. Add onion and cook until translucent, stirring occasionally, about 10 minutes. Add spinach and sauté 3 minutes.

Set aside ¼ cup egg mixture. Blend remaining egg mixture into spinach. Spoon on top of pie. Pour reserved egg mixture over. Bake until custard is set and top is golden brown, 25 to 30 minutes. Let stand 30 minutes. Remove springform. Cut pie into slices.

MEAT AND POULTRY

MEAT AND POULTRY

CHICKEN WITH BRIE AND PECANS

An elegant and surprisingly easy-to-prepare entree. Serve with "White Wine Salad."

4 chicken breasts, boned and skinned
¼ cup flour seasoned with salt and pepper
4 tablespoons butter or margarine
1 tablespoon oil
½ cup dry white wine
½ cup cream
4 to 6 ounces Brie, cut into ½-inch nuggets
½ cup pecans, toasted at 350° for 10 minutes

Serves 4.

Place chicken between plastic wrap and pound to ¼ to ½-inch thickness. Dip each breast in seasoned flour. Heat 10-inch skillet. Add butter and oil. When foaming, add chicken. Cook 1 to 2 minutes on each side. Add wine and cream to pan. Cover and simmer 4 to 5 minutes. Remove chicken and check for doneness. Allow liquid to reduce to ½ cup over high heat. Reduce heat so sauce simmers. Add Brie and shake the pan over heat until cheese is melted and sauce is smooth. Place on a heated serving platter. Add pecans to sauce and spoon over chicken. Garnish with a few pecans if desired.

HERB CHICKEN IN PHYLLO

An extravagantly delicious combination of classics.

2 tablespoons minced watercress, optional
1½ teaspoons fresh tarragon, minced or
½ teaspoon dried tarragon
½ cup butter or margarine, softened
4 boneless chicken breasts, halved with skin removed
6 tablespoons butter or margarine
8 sheets phyllo, fresh or frozen and thawed
Salt
Pepper
Fresh tarragon sprigs for garnish, optional

Champagne Sauce:
1 tablespoon butter or margarine
1 shallot, minced
½ cup Champagne or sparkling white wine
1 cup heavy or whipping cream
⅛ teaspoon salt

Serves 8.

About 1½ hours before serving, mix watercress, tarragon and butter or margarine until blended together in a small bowl. Cover and refrigerate.

Using meat mallet, pound each chicken breast half to ½-inch thickness. With a knife, slice open each breast so you will form a small pocket. Place 1 tablespoon of tarragon butter in each pocket. Press closed.

In 1-quart saucepan over low heat melt 6 tablespoons butter or margarine. On work surface, place 1 sheet phyllo. Brush lightly with melted butter or margarine. Fold in half to form rectangle. Place a chicken breast half in center of phyllo with long side of chicken parallel to folded edge. Sprinkle chicken lightly with salt and pepper. Bring sides of phyllo up and over chicken, covering completely, pinching edges together at top to form a ruffled edge. Place chicken phyllo packets in 2 jelly roll pans, brushing with butter or margarine. Bake at 400° for 20 minutes or until tender and golden.

To make sauce, melt butter or margarine in a 3-quart saucepan. Saute shallot until tender. Increasing heat to medium high, add Champagne or white wine. Heat to boiling. Boil for 5 minutes. Reduce heat to medium, stir in cream and salt. Heat to boiling. Boil for 2 minutes and serve sauce in a gravy boat and chicken arranged on platter.

SAUTEED CHICKEN BREASTS WITH MARSALA

Serve Fettuccine Alfredo and a Chardonnay with this entree.

4 chicken breasts, boned and skinned
Salt
Freshly ground black pepper
Flour for dredging
2 tablespoons unsalted butter
3 tablespoons olive oil
½ cup dry Marsala
½ cup chicken broth
2 tablespoons soft unsalted butter

Serves 4 to 6.

Remove white tendon from boned, skinned chicken breasts. If necessary, slice very thick pieces of breast meat horizontally into two fillets. Pound all pieces to ¼-inch thickness. Season with salt and pepper, and dredge in flour.

In large, heavy skillet, melt 2 tablespoons butter and 3 tablespoons oil over medium high heat. When foam subsides, add the chicken pieces 3 or 4 at a time. Do not overcrowd the pan. Brown them for about 3 minutes on each side. After they have browned, transfer to a plate. Continue with remaining chicken.

Pour off most of the fat from the pan, leaving a thin film on the bottom. Add Marsala and ¼ cup chicken broth and boil liquid rapidly over high heat for 1 to 2 minutes. Scrape any browned fragments clinging to the pan into sauce. Return all the browned chicken to the pan, cover and simmer over low heat for 10 to 15 minutes, basting occasionally with the pan juices.

Transfer chicken to a heated serving platter, covering with foil to retain heat. Add ¼ cup chicken broth to sauce in pan and boil rapidly. When reduced to a syrupy glaze, taste for seasoning. Remove pan from heat, stir in 2 tablespoons soft butter and pour sauce over the chicken and serve.

DUNGENESS STUFFED CHICKEN BREASTS

Sauce:
3 tablespoons butter
¼ cup flour
⅔ cup milk
1 cup hot chicken stock or broth
⅓ cup dry white wine
Salt

Filling:
2 tablespoons butter
5 green onions, minced
8 large fresh mushrooms, cleaned and chopped
1-pound fresh Dungeness crab meat
½ cup crushed soda crackers
¼ cup parsley, snipped
½ teaspoon salt
Pepper

Chicken Rolls:
4 large whole chicken breasts, boned, skinned and halved
1½ cups Swiss cheese, shredded
Paprika

Serves 8 to 10.

To prepare sauce: Melt the butter in a saucepan, stir in the flour and cook over low heat about 3 minutes, stirring constantly.

Add the milk, chicken stock and wine and stir to blend well. Bring to a boil, turn heat to low and simmer about 3 minutes longer, stirring until thick. Season to taste with salt.

To prepare filling: Melt the butter in a skillet and saute the onion and mushrooms until the onion is soft. Stir in ½ pound crab meat, cracker crumbs, parsley, salt and pepper. Stir in 3 tablespoons of the sauce.

To prepare rolls: Using the side of a meat mallet, flatten chicken breasts between two sheets of wax paper until as thin as possible.

Place ¼ cup filling mixture on each breast. Bring sides up over the filling and roll up chicken, covering all filling. Place chicken rolls seam side down in a 7-by-11-inch baking dish.

Stir remaining ½-pound crab meat into the remaining sauce. Pour sauce over chicken. Bake, covered, 1 hour at 350°. Remove from oven, uncover and sprinkle cheese and paprika over the top. Bake 5 minutes longer.

PICNIC CHICKEN

Oven-baked chicken — an effortless and savory way to create a picnic.

2 to 3 pounds chicken pieces, skinned
1 cup sour cream
3 tablespoons lemon juice
1 large clove garlic, minced
¼ teaspoon tabasco
Salt to taste
Pepper to taste
2 cups crushed soda crackers
2 teaspoons thyme
2 teaspoons dry mustard
1 teaspoon paprika
¼ teaspoon cayenne
¼ cup melted butter or margarine

Serves 6 to 8.

Mix together sour cream, lemon juice, garlic, tabasco, salt and pepper. Skin 2 to 3 pounds of chicken pieces and marinate overnight in mixture.

Mix together crackers, thyme, mustard, paprika and cayenne. Coat chicken pieces.

Butter pan. Drizzle chicken with melted butter. Bake for 45 minutes at 375°.

PARMESAN YOGURT CHICKEN

Cayenne pepper adds "snap" to this dish.

3 to 4 chicken breasts
2 tablespoons lemon juice
Salt and pepper
½ cup unflavored yogurt
¼ cup mayonnaise
1 tablespoon Dijon mustard
1 tablespoon Worcestershire sauce
½ teaspoon ground thyme
¼ teaspoon cayenne pepper
¼ cup green onion, thinly sliced
½ cup grated Parmesan cheese

Serves 4.

Pull skin off chicken and any excess fat. Place in baking dish. Squeeze lemon juice over chicken and season lightly with salt and pepper. Combine remaining ingredients and mix well. Spread evenly over chicken pieces.

Bake uncovered at 350° for 1 hour. Chicken will be golden brown. Use drippings to drizzle over rice that will accompany.

BARBEQUED CHICKEN WITH HONEY MUSTARD GLAZE

The unusual marinade creates the tangy glaze.

1 8-ounce can tomato sauce
½ cup olive oil
½ cup orange juice
¼ cup vinegar
1½ teaspoons dried oregano, crushed
1 teaspoon salt
6 peppercorns
1 garlic clove, minced
2 whole chicken breasts, split
4 chicken legs and thighs
¼ cup honey
½ teaspoon dry mustard

Serves 6 to 8.

In a 1-quart screw-top jar, combine all ingredients except chicken, honey and mustard. Cover jar and shake vigorously to blend. In shallow dish, pour tomato sauce mixture over chicken and marinate 2 hours at room temperature or overnight in refrigerator, turning occasionally. Drain, reserving marinade. Grill chicken over medium coals for 45 to 60 minutes, brushing with marinade and turning frequently. Combine honey and mustard together. Just before serving, brush chicken with honey mustard glaze.

CASHEW CHICKEN

1 egg white
2 tablespoons cornstarch
1 tablespoon oil
1 teaspoon soy sauce
1 teaspoon rice wine or saki
⅛ teaspoon salt
Dash of pepper
½ pound boneless chicken breast, diced
5 tablespoons oil
Dash of red chili pepper flakes, optional
2 green onions, minced
⅛ to ¼ teaspoon fresh ginger root, grated
2 tablespoons soy sauce
1 tablespoon rice vinegar
1 tablespoon rice wine
1 tablespoon sugar
1 teaspoon cornstarch mixed with
2 tablespoons water
¼ cup raw cashews, unsalted

Serves 2 to 4.

To make marinade, combine egg white, cornstarch, oil, soy sauce, rice wine or saki, salt and pepper. Soak chicken in marinade for 15 to 60 minutes.

In wok, heat oil over high heat. When oil is heated, reduce heat to medium-high. Being careful not to splatter, add dash of red pepper, chicken, green onions, ginger and soy sauce. Stir gently with chopsticks or wooden spatula to prevent chicken from burning or sticking to bottom of wok.

After chicken turns white, add soy sauce, vinegar, wine, sugar and cornstarch mixture. When mixture thickens and chicken is warmed thoroughly, add cashews. Heat slightly and serve immediately.

CHICKEN SZECHUAN

Sauce:
4 tablespoons light soy sauce
1 tablespoon sugar
1 tablespoon dry sherry wine

Chicken:
2 boneless chicken breasts, skins removed
1 egg white
1 tablespoon cornstarch
4 tablespoons vegetable oil
1 tablespoon or less red pepper flakes
1 cup dry roasted peanuts
3 green onions, cut into 2-inch pieces

Serves 4.

In small bowl, whisk sauce ingredients together. Slice chicken breasts into strips and combine with egg white and cornstarch. Heat oil in wok. Stir fry pepper flakes 10 seconds. Add chicken and stir fry until white. Stir in sauce. Add the peanuts and green onions. Serve.

ROCK CORNISH GAME HENS HAWAIIAN

Take a trip to the Islands with this uniquely sweetened approach to game hens.

4 Cornish game hens
2 tablespoons honey
1 teaspoon soy sauce
¼ cup juice drained from canned pineapple
¼ cup canned crushed pineapple, drained
1 small onion, minced
1 cup packaged stuffing croutons
⅛ teaspoon thyme
Salt to taste
Pepper to taste
Water

Serves 4.

Mix together pineapple, onion, butter, croutons, thyme, salt, pepper and enough hot water to moisten. Stuff game hens and roast for 1 to 1½ hours at 350°. Mix honey, soy sauce and pineapple juice in small saucepan and heat. Baste game hens as they bake.

ROAST BEEF TERIYAKI

6 to 7 pound beef rib roast
2 cups beef broth
⅔ cup Japanese soy sauce
½ cup red wine
3 tablespoons brown sugar
2 tablespoons lemon juice
2 teaspoons powdered ginger
2 cloves garlic, crushed
6 green onions, sliced

Serves 8-10.

Place meat in deep bowl. Mix together broth, soy sauce, wine, green onions, sugar, lemon juice, ginger, and garlic. Stir marinade until sugar dissolves. Pour over meat. Let marinate in refrigerator at least 10 hours. Turn occasionally.

Remove meat from marinade. Place on rack in FOIL LINED roasting pan. Pour marinade into saucepan, set aside. Cook meat at 325° for 20 to 25 minutes per pound for medium rare. Brush meat with marinade while roasting. Let stand for 20 minutes before serving. Heat marinade and serve in sauceboat with meal.

BAKED STUFFED FLANK STEAK ROLL

The flavorful marinade enhances the meat's flavor along with the bake-alongside potatoes and mushroom dressing.

Marinade:
¼ cup lemon juice
¼ cup soy sauce
¼ cup honey
1 teaspoon dry mustard
½ teaspoon pepper
2 pound flank steak
6 medium russet potatoes, scrubbed and pierced with a fork
2 cups beef broth, regular strength
2 tablespoons cornstarch
Parsley or mint sprigs, optional

Mushroom Stuffing:
1 pound mushrooms
1 medium onion, chopped
¼ cup butter or margarine
½ cup parsley, chopped

Serves 6.

In a 9 by 13-inch baking pan, mix together lemon juice, soy sauce, honey, dry mustard and pepper. Lay flank steak in sauce and turn over to coat all sides of meat. Cover with plastic wrap and refrigerate at least 1 hour or until the next day, turning meat several times. Lift steak from marinade. Brush excess sauce off meat into pan.

To prepare mushroom stuffing, rinse, drain and thinly slice mushrooms. Chop onion. Melt butter in a 10 to 12-inch frying pan over medium-high heat. Add vegetables and cook, stirring occasionally, until golden brown or about 25 minutes. Stir in chopped parsley. Let cool. If making ahead, cover and chill overnight.

Lay steak flat. Spoon mushroom stuffing onto center of the steak and across its width. Fold steak ends over the stuffing to overlap completely. With cotton string, tie the rolled meat in the center and at each end to hold securely. Place rolled steak, seam down, in the pan with the marinade. Cover tightly with foil. If making ahead, chill until next day.

Bake in the center of oven at 350° until meat is very tender when pierced, about 3 hours. About 1 hour before steak is done, add potatoes to oven on rack above meat. Bake until tender when pierced. Using 2 spoons, carefully lift rolled steak and place seam down on a platter. Clip and remove strings. Cover meat with foil and keep warm.

Carefully skim and discard fat from pan drippings. Stir broth and cornstarch into the pan. Stirring, bring the mixture to a boil over high heat. Pour into a sauceboat.

Cut rolled steak crosswise into 6 equal slices. Arrange meat and potatoes on plates, garnish with parsley and add sauce to taste.

COMPANY BEST BEEF BOURGUIGNONNE

8 slices bacon
3 pounds stew meat, fat removed
2 10¾-ounce cans beefy mushroom soup
2 cups burgundy or dry red wine
4 tablespoons tomato paste
½ teaspoon thyme leaves
2 medium bay leaves
3 medium cloves garlic, minced
16 small whole white onions, about 1 pound or 1 package frozen white onions
4 medium carrots, cut into 2-inch strips
½ cup parsley, chopped

Serves 8 to 12.

In Dutch oven, cook bacon until crisp. Remove and crumble. In batches, brown beef in drippings. Add soup, wine, tomato paste, crumbled bacon, beef, garlic and seasonings. Cover and bake 2 hours at 350°, stirring occasionally.

Preferably overnight, chill and remove hardened fat. Remove bay leaves. If desired, beef can be frozen at this point. Add onions and carrots. Cook 1 hour or until done.

Sprinkle with chopped parsley and serve over noodles.

BUTTERFLIED LEG OF LAMB

Serve with lemon rice pilaf and mint jelly.

2 tablespoons Dijon mustard
½ teaspoon salt
¼ teaspoon pepper
4 tablespoons brown sugar
2 tablespoons soy sauce
2 tablespoons olive oil
1 garlic clove, crushed
⅓ cup lemon juice
4 to 5 pound leg of lamb, butterflied

Serves 8.

Combine mustard, salt, pepper, brown sugar, soy sauce, olive oil, garlic and lemon juice together mixing well. Bone and flatten lamb or have butcher do it. Brush lamb with sauce and roast in 450° oven for 35 minutes. Brush and baste frequently.

Allow to rest before carving. Slice thinly on bias as you would a London Broil.

ROSEMARY LEG OF LAMB

1 leg of lamb, well trimmed of fat
Salt
¼ cup parsley, finely chopped
3 tablespoons fresh rosemary
or 1 tablespoon dried rosemary
1 tablespoon olive oil
2 garlic cloves, crushed
¼ teaspoon salt
1¼ cups chicken broth
New potatoes

Rub lamb with salt. In thickest part of meat, make 6 or 7 deep cuts. Combine ingredients except broth. Gently push mixture into cuts. Spread any leftover mixture over surface of meat.

Roast for 2½ hours at 325°. Baste frequently with chicken broth.

Serve with pan roasted new potatoes.

LAMB AVGOLEMONO

3 pounds lean shoulder of lamb, boned and cut into 3-inch pieces
Salt
Pepper
Garlic powder
2 tablespoons olive oil
2 tablespoons butter
3 medium onions, chopped
2 tablespoons flour
½ cup water
½ cup white wine
2 teaspoons dried dill weed
2 tablespoons fresh parsley, minced
¾ teaspoon salt
1 bunch celery
3 medium zucchini
4 egg yolks
6 tablespoons lemon juice

Serves 6.

Sprinkle lamb with salt, pepper and garlic powder. Heat oil in large pan. Brown meat on all sides. Remove. Add butter to pan and cook onions over moderate heat until wilted. Blend in flour. Add water and cook, stirring until thick and smooth. Add wine. Return meat to pan. Add dill, parsley and salt. Simmer covered for one hour.

Slice celery diagonally into 1-inch pieces. Chop half the leaves. Scrape zucchini, but do not peel. Slice diagonally into 2-inch pieces. Add zucchini, celery and leaves to stew. Cover and cook for 10 minutes. If desired, stew can be frozen at this point.

To serve, reheat over low heat about 45 minutes or until hot.

When ready to serve, beat egg yolks until thick. Beat in lemon juice 1 tablespoon at a time. Gradually stir in 1 cup hot liquid from stew. Slowly pour egg mixture into stew, stirring into hot sauce until well mixed.

Serve with rice pilaf, mixed with canned garbanzo beans, which have been sauteed with chopped onion.

ROAST PORK WITH ONION AND MUSTARD SAUCE

Homemade applesauce or an apple salad, make perfect companions for this pork dish.

1½ teaspoons paprika
1 teaspoon salt
1 teaspoon marjoram
½ teaspoon thyme
¼ teaspoon pepper
1 large clove garlic, crushed
3 to 3½ pound boneless pork loin top roast, (or a bone-in pork loin roast)
1½ cups full-strength canned beef broth
1½ cups water
5 to 8 medium red or white new potatoes, scrubbed and cut into quarters
6 carrots, scrubbed and cut into one-inch pieces
1 to 2 medium onions, chopped
2 tablespoons butter or margarine
1 to 2 tablespoons flour
1 tablespoon Dijon mustard
1 cup half-and-half

Serves 6.

Mix paprika, salt, marjoram, thyme, pepper and garlic together and rub over roast. Place pork in a large roasting pan. Add vegetables. Pour beef broth and water into the pan. Cook uncovered, 30 minutes per pound at 350°, basting every half hour.

Approximately 45 minutes before serving, saute chopped onions in butter or margarine over low heat until soft or about 30 minutes. In a small bowl, mix flour and mustard. Gradually stir in cream.

Remove pork from pan and let stand uncut. Skim fat from pan juices and discard. Add onions and cream mixture. Boil, stirring constantly until smooth and thickened. Add an extra 2 tablespoons of flour to thicken if needed. Taste and adjust seasoning.

Arrange sliced pork with potatoes and carrots on a platter. Serve with sauce.

CROWN PORK ROAST WITH SWEET AND SOUR ORANGE SAUCE

A spectacular Autumn dinner entree.

Roast:
10-pound crown pork roast, custom cut strip of pork loin, backbone removed
2 cups fresh orange juice, reserve half orange peels in plastic bag in refrigerator for garnish when serving
¼ cup honey
2 tablespoons brown sugar
1 teaspoon lemon juice
2 cloves garlic, crushed
½ teaspoon dry mustard
2 tablespoons cornstarch mixed with ¼ cup cold water

Apple Stuffing:
2 cups diced apple
5 cups toasted bread cubes
½ cup raisins, soaked
½ cup prunes, cooked and chopped (optional)
½ cup butter, melted
4 tablespoons light brown sugar
2 teaspoons lemon peel, grated
½ teaspoon paprika
½ teaspoon cinnamon
½ cup apple juice
1 teaspoon salt

Pour orange juice into saucepan. Add honey, brown sugar, lemon juice, garlic, dry mustard and cornstarch solution. Place pan over medium heat and stir until thickened.

Marinate meat overnight in sauce.

To roast, place in roasting pan, bone ends up. Wrap tips to prevent excess browning. Salt and pepper roast. Roast uncovered in slow oven at 325° until thermometer reads 185° or about 50 to 55 minutes for each pound of meat. One hour before meat is done, fill center with stuffing. To prepare stuffing, combine ingredients together. Bake remaining stuffing in greased casserole and dot with butter. Cover and bake with roast for last hour.

Baste roast with marinade sauce during last 20 minutes of cooking time. Continue basting while roast cools.

To serve, replace foil ends with spiced apples or paper frills. To carve, slice between ribs.

If stuffing isn't used, place roast in pan, bone end down so fat from roast bastes rib ends. At serving time fill roast with roast potatoes or other vegetables.

To prepare orange garnish, dry orange halves in oven at 225° for 40 to 50 minutes. Fill oranges with vegetables being served and set around meat.

LOIN OF PORK WITH PORT SAUCE

A tasty buffet entree — serve with "Brandied Carrots."

4 to 5 pound pork loin
1 tablespoon Dijon style mustard
½ teaspoon salt
¼ teaspoon dried thyme leaves
¼ teaspoon pepper
½ cup tawny-colored port
¼ cup soy sauce
3 cloves garlic, minced
2 teaspoons ground ginger

Port Sauce:
1 10-ounce jar red currant jelly
2 tablespoons tawny port
1 tablespoon soy sauce
2 tablespoons lemon juice

Serves 8 to 10.

Rub pork with mustard, salt, thyme, and pepper. Place in large baking dish. Mix ½ cup port, ¼ cup soy sauce, garlic and ginger. Pour over meat. Refrigerate overnight.

Roast meat uncovered at 325°, baste often with marinade. Cook until tender (meat thermometer 170°) 2½ to 3 hours.

Heat jelly, port, and soy sauce to boiling. Boil for five minutes and stir in lemon juice.

Pour jelly mixture over meat. Let stand at room temperature for 1 hour. Baste with jelly several times. Remove meat to serving plate. Strain jelly mixture and pour over meat.

PORK PICADILLO

A surprising combination of flavors. Serve this hearty entree over rice.

1 large onion, finely chopped
2 tablespoons butter
2 tablespoons olive oil
3½ pounds boneless pork, cut in ¾-inch cubes
2 garlic cloves, minced
2 8-ounce cans tomato sauce
½ cup tomato-based chili sauce
1 teaspoon cinnamon
1 teaspoon salt
¼ teaspoon ground cumin
½ cup raisins
3 tablespoons vinegar
3 tablespoons brown sugar
2 green limes
2 green onions

Serves 6.

Using a deep, heavy pot, saute onion in 1 tablespoon each of butter and oil. Remove onion from pan into bowl. In heavy pot add remaining oil and butter. Brown meat, a little at a time. Return onion to pan. Add garlic, tomato sauce, chili sauce, cinnamon, salt, cumin, raisins, vinegar and brown sugar. Cover and simmer 1 hour, or until meat is tender. Stir occasionally and add a little water if sauce seems too thick. Serve immediately or refrigerate and serve next day. To reheat, place in 350° oven for 45 minutes.

Serve over rice and garnish meat with thinly sliced green onion. Serve with lime wedges to squeeze over top.

ASPARAGUS AND HAM ROLL-UPS

A satisfying summer luncheon entree with fresh asparagus. Serve with mandarin salad.

16 medium asparagus spears, trimmed and peeled
½ teaspoon unsalted butter
1 large shallot, minced
1 teaspoon Dijon mustard
2 tablespoons heavy or whipping cream
½ teaspoon lemon juice
½ pound boiled ham, thinly sliced
3 tablespoons Parmesan cheese, freshly grated
½ pound Fontina cheese, coarsely grated
Black pepper, freshly ground

Serves 4.

Blanch asparagus and drain on paper towels.

Melt butter in small skillet over medium-low heat. Add shallot and saute until lightly browned. Remove from the heat and stir in the mustard, cream and lemon juice, blending well.

Spread small amount of shallot-mustard mixture over each slice of ham. Sprinkle each piece with Parmesan cheese. Divide Fontina cheese into halves. Sprinkle one half evenly over ham slices.

Place two asparagus spears in center of each ham slice. Fold ham over asparagus and arrange in a lightly greased ovenproof serving dish, seam-side down. Sprinkle with remaining Fontina cheese and black pepper. Bake until lightly browned and bubbly at 400° for 15 to 20 minutes.

THE MAIN DISH

THE MAIN DISH

VEAL CANNELLONI WITH CREAM SAUCE

Sauce:
4 tablespoons butter
4 tablespoons flour
½ teaspoon salt
⅛ teaspoon white pepper
⅛ teaspoon grated nutmeg
2 cups milk
4 tablespoons tomato sauce
¼ cup cream

Filling:
2 tablespoons olive oil
3 tablespoons onion, minced
3 tablespoons celery, finely chopped
2 tablespoons carrot, finely chopped
1 tablespoon parsley, minced
2 cups cooked veal or chicken, ground or finely chopped
¾ teaspoon salt
¼ teaspoon each, dried oregano and basil
White pepper
¾ cup dry white wine

Cannelloni sheets, 4″ x 6″
Parmesan cheese, grated

Serves 4.

To prepare sauce, melt butter in saucepan. Stir in flour and seasonings. Allow mixture to cook, bubbling for 2 to 3 minutes, stirring constantly. Do not burn! Add milk, stirring constantly until sauce is smooth and thick. Cook for additional 5 minutes.

To prepare filling, sauté vegetables in olive oil for 10 minutes. Add remaining ingredients and simmer until wine is reduced by half. Stir in ½ cup of sauce.

To make cannelloni, cook 8 cannelloni sheets in boiling salted water until al dente. Drain, rinse in cold water, pat dry. Put 2 tablespoons filling on each cannelloni and roll up. Arrange filled cannelloni in a 10 x 14-inch buttered au gratin dish or similar pan. Add tomato sauce and cream to remaining sauce. Stir to blend. Pour ½ cup of this sauce over each serving and sprinkle with freshly grated Parmesan cheese.

Bake at 450° for 10 minutes or until top browns. Serve immediately with freshly ground Parmesan cheese on the side.

CRAB AND SHRIMP CANNELLONI

An unforgettable company dish. Prepare the day before serving and you've got no-fuss entertaining!

Tomato Sauce:
2 tablespoons butter or margarine
1 medium onion, finely chopped
1 medium carrot, shredded
¼ cup chopped parsley
1 can (about 1 lb.) tomatoes
1 cup chicken broth
1 teaspoon dry basil

Filling:
¾ pound cooked or canned crab, flaked
½ pound small cooked shrimp
3 green onions (including tops), thinly sliced
1 cup (4-ounces) fontina cheese, shredded
16 unfilled cannelloni
Boiling salted water
½ cup Parmesan cheese, freshly grated

White Sauce:
½ cup butter or margarine
1 small onion, finely chopped
4 tablespoons all-purpose flour
⅛ teaspoon nutmeg, ground
⅛ teaspoon white pepper
¾ cup milk
¾ cup chicken broth
1 cup (4-ounces) fontina cheese, shredded
2 tablespoons dry vermouth

Serves 8.

To make tomato sauce, melt butter in a wide frying pan over medium-high heat. Add onion and carrot and cook until onion is limp and lightly browned. Add parsley, tomatoes and their liquid (break up tomatoes with a spoon), chicken broth, and basil. Bring to a boil, reduce heat, cover, and simmer for 15 minutes. Uncover and continue cooking, stirring occasionally, until sauce is thickened (about 30 minutes).

To make filling, combine crab, shrimp, green onions, and fontina; mix lightly.

Cook fresh or frozen pasta, 4 or 5 rectangles at a time, in a large kettle of boiling salted water until al dente (2 to 3 minutes). Remove with a slotted spoon, rinse with cold water, and drain. When all pasta is cooked, fill by placing about ¼ cup crab filling in a row along one long edge of each rectangle; roll to enclose filling.

To make white sauce, melt butter in a 2-quart pan over medium heat. Add onion and cook until limp. Blend in flour, nutmeg, and pepper. Remove pan from heat and gradually stir in milk and chicken broth. Return to heat and cook, stirring constantly, until sauce is smooth and thickened. Stir in fontina until melted. Mix in vermouth.

Spread tomato sauce in a buttered 9 × 13-inch baking pan. Place filled cannelloni, seam side down and slightly apart, in sauce. Pour white sauce evenly over cannelloni. Sprinkle with Parmesan.

Bake, uncovered, in a 400° oven until hot and bubbly and cheese is lightly browned (30 to 35 minutes).

HAM AND CHICKEN CANNELLONI WITH SAUCE

Sauce:
¼ cup butter
1 clove garlic, crushed
¼ cup flour
1½ teaspoon powdered chicken bouillon
⅛ teaspoon white pepper
2 cups light cream or half and half
½ cup combined grated Parmesan and Romano cheese

Cannelloni:
6 cannelloni shells
2 tablespoons butter
3 tablespoons green onions, sliced
1 10-ounce package frozen spinach, thawed and well-drained
1 cup cooked chicken, finely chopped
1 cup cooked ham, finely chopped
½ cup combined grated Parmesan and Romano cheese
2 eggs, beaten
¾ teaspoon Italian seasoning
¼ teaspoon pepper

Serves 4.

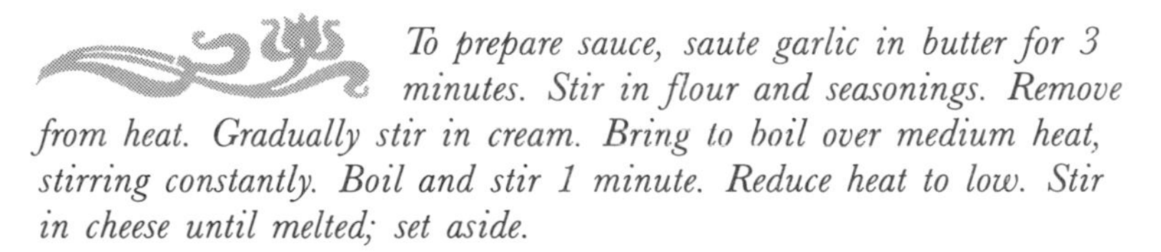

To prepare sauce, saute garlic in butter for 3 minutes. Stir in flour and seasonings. Remove from heat. Gradually stir in cream. Bring to boil over medium heat, stirring constantly. Boil and stir 1 minute. Reduce heat to low. Stir in cheese until melted; set aside.

To make cannelloni, parboil shells according to package directions. Rinse and drain. Saute onion in butter about 3 minutes. Remove from heat; stir in remaining ingredients. Fill shells. Place in buttered baking dish. Spoon sauce over filled cannelloni. Bake 20 minutes at 350°. Broil several inches from heat source until sauce is golden brown and bubbles, about 5 minutes.

Serve immediately.

SPINACH AND CHEESE CANNELLONI

A savory meatless entrée that you can assemble up to eight hours prior to cooking.

16 large cannelloni
2 cups white sauce

Spinach and Cheese Filling:
1 lb. spinach, stemmed, parboiled for 2 minutes, squeezed dry and chopped
10-ounces ricotta cheese
2⅓ cups Parmesan cheese, freshly grated
5-ounces mascarpone or crescenza cheese
Salt and freshly ground pepper
Nutmeg, freshly grated

Serves 4.

Put plenty of salted water on to boil for the pasta. When the water boils, put in the cannelloni one at a time, stir and cook over medium heat. When the cannelloni are half-cooked (5 or 6 minutes for commercial pasta or 2 minutes for fresh pasta), remove them and plunge them into cold water. Then drain them and spread them out on cloth towels.

While the pasta is cooking, put the chopped spinach into a bowl with the ricotta, about half of the Parmesan, the mascarpone or crescenza, and a pinch each of salt, pepper and nutmeg. Mix well.

Thoroughly butter an ovenproof dish large enough to hold the cannelloni in a single layer. Fill the cannelloni with the spinach and cheese mixture and arrange them in the dish. Sprinkle with the rest of the Parmesan and cover with the white sauce. Bake, uncovered, at 350° for 20 minutes or until the sauce is bubbling and surface is lightly colored.

FRESH VEGETABLE LASAGNE

Not only will your vegetarian friends love this tempting lasagne, they'll beg you for the recipe.

2 tablespoons olive oil
1 large onion, chopped
1 large green pepper, cut into slivers
2 cloves garlic, minced
5 medium tomatoes, diced, peeled and drained
2 teaspoons dried leaf oregano
1 tablespoon fresh basil, chopped or
1 teaspoon dried basil
1 teaspoon salt
¼ teaspoon pepper
4 eggs
1 large eggplant, unpeeled, sliced ½-inch thick
⅔ cup seasoned, dry bread crumbs
2 cups ricotta cheese
¼ cup Parmesan cheese, freshly grated
8-ounces Monterey Jack cheese,
shredded or thinly sliced

Serves 6 to 8.

In a large saucepan, heat oil. Saute onion, green pepper and garlic until tender. Stir in tomatoes, oregano, basil, salt and pepper. Cover. Simmer 35 to 40 minutes stirring occasionally.

In a shallow dish, beat 2 eggs until foamy. Dip eggplant slices in eggs, then in bread crumbs. Arrange slices on a lightly oiled baking sheet. Bake for 20 to 25 minutes at 350°.

Spread about 1 cup of the tomato sauce in a 9 x 13-inch baking dish. Cover with half the eggplant slices.

In a small bowl, lightly beat remaining 2 eggs. Stir in ricotta cheese. Spoon half the cheese mixture over the eggplant. Sprinkle with 2 tablespoons Parmesan cheese, half the Jack cheese and 1 cup of the tomato sauce. Repeat layers ending with Jack cheese on top. Bake at 375° for 30 to 35 minutes until hot and bubbly. Let stand 10 minutes before serving.

SEAFOOD LASAGNE

A rich and creamy showcase for shellfish.

Seafood Sauce:
3 tablespoons olive oil
1 large yellow onion, chopped
4 cloves garlic, minced
5 cups canned plum tomatoes (packed in tomato purée)
½ cup dry white wine
½ cup fresh basil, chopped
2 teaspoons fennel seeds
Salt and freshly ground black pepper, to taste
1 cup heavy or whipping cream
2 tablespoons Pernod
1 pound medium-size shrimp, shelled, deveined, and poached briefly
1 pound scallops, poached briefly
3 dozen mussels, steamed and shelled
2 dozen littleneck clams, steamed and shelled

1¼ pounds lasagne noodles, preferably fresh tomato noodles

Filling:
3 cups ricotta cheese
8-ounces cream cheese, room temperature
2 eggs
1 package (10 ounces) spinach, cooked, drained, and chopped
1 pound cooked lump crabmeat, shredded
1 sweet red pepper, seeded, cored, and diced
1 bunch scallions (green onions), sliced
½ cup fresh basil, chopped
Salt and freshly ground black pepper, to taste

1½ pounds mozzarella cheese, thinly sliced

Serves 10 to 12.

To make the seafood sauce, heat the oil in a large skillet over medium-high heat. Add the onion and garlic and sauté for 5 minutes. Add the tomatoes with the purée and cook for 5 minutes more. Stir in the wine, basil, fennel seeds, and salt and pepper to taste. Simmer uncovered over medium heat for 45 minutes, stirring occasionally.

Stir the cream into the sauce and then the Pernod. Stir in all the shellfish and simmer 5 minutes. Remove from heat.

Cook the lasagne noodles in boiling salted water until tender but still firm. Drain and cool under cold running water.

To make the filling, beat the ricotta, cream cheese, and eggs in a mixing bowl with a wooden spoon until smooth. Stir in the spinach, crabmeat, red pepper, scallions, basil, and salt and pepper to taste.

Butter a large rectangular baking pan. Spread a thin layer of the sauce without any shellfish on the bottom of the pan. Cover with a layer of noodles. Top with half the filling, then half the seafood sauce. Cover the sauce with a layer of mozzarella.

Place another layer of noodles over the mozzarella and spread with the remaining filling. Top with another layer of mozzarella. Add a final layer of noodles and then the remaining seafood sauce. Cover with the remaining cheese.

Bake the lasagne at 350° until bubbling and browned, about 50 minutes. Let stand for 10 minutes before serving.

PASTA PRIMAVERA

A great way to showcase your garden's bounty. Fresh basil adds the perfect touch.

½ cup unsalted butter
1 bunch green onions, thinly sliced
1 large clove garlic, minced
1 pound thin asparagus, with tough ends removed, cut diagonally into 1-inch slices, tips intact
½ pound mushrooms, thinly sliced
6 ounces cauliflower, broken into small flowerets
1 medium zucchini, cut julienne
1 small carrot, cut julienne
1 cup whipping cream
½ cup chicken broth
2 tablespoons fresh or 2 teaspoons dried basil
8-ounces fresh Chinese pea pods
4-ounces cooked ham, chopped
8 cherry tomatoes, cut in half
Salt and freshly ground pepper
1 pound fettuccine cooked al dente and thoroughly drained
1 cup Parmesan cheese, freshly grated

Serves 6 to 8.

Heat wok or large deep skillet over medium high heat. Add butter, onion and garlic and saute until onion is softened (about 2 minutes). Mix in asparagus, mushrooms, cauliflower, zucchini and carrot and stir fry 2 minutes.

Increase heat to high. Add cream, broth and basil and allow mixture to boil until liquid is slightly reduced (about 3 minutes). Stir in pea pods and ham and cook 1 minute more. Season with salt and pepper.

Add pasta and cheese, tossing until thoroughly combined and pasta is heated through. Turn onto large serving platter and garnish with cherry tomatoes. Serve immediately.

Serve with a leafy green salad and French bread.

FETTUCCINE WITH CHEVRE' CHEESE AND SMOKED SALMON

An effortless and impressive entree — prepared in just 15 minutes!

1 pint whipping or heavy cream
6 to 8-ounces Chevre' or Brie cheese
½ pound smoked salmon
1 pound fettuccine noodles
Fresh parsley to garnish

Serves 4 to 6.

In a saucepan over medium to low heat, stir the whipping cream until heated, but not boiling. Blend in cheese. When melted, crumble in salmon. Keep stirring to prevent cream from scorching. When thickened, pour over fettuccine, cooked according to package directions. Garnish with parsley.

MEXICAN CHICKEN ROLLS

This wonderful entree is well-worth the time and effort. Serve with a simple avocado salad, rice, and pineapple spears.

2 whole chicken breasts, split, skinned and boned
1 4-ounce can whole green chili peppers
4 teaspoons pitted black olives, chopped
½ cup Monterey Jack cheese, shredded
1 egg, slightly beaten
1 cup crushed tortilla chips
¼ cup vegetable oil
1 1.5-ounce envelope enchilada sauce mix
½ cup water
1 16-ounce can Mexican-style stewed tomatoes
½ cup Cheddar cheese, shredded

Serves 4.

Pound chicken breasts to flatten. On each breast, put 1 chili pepper, 1 teaspoon olives and 2 tablespoons Monterey Jack cheese. Roll up the breasts tightly and secure with toothpicks. Dip each roll into the egg, then into chips to coat. Heat oil in skillet and brown chicken rolls lightly. Place rolls in a shallow casserole dish. Prepare enchilada sauce according to package directions, using only ½ cup water and Mexican-style tomatoes. Pour sauce over chicken rolls. Bake at 350° for 35 to 40 minutes. Sprinkle top of chicken with Cheddar cheese and bake an additional 5 minutes or until cheese is bubbly.

ENCHILADAS

Who would think of using cinnamon and peanut butter in enchiladas? This one will yield you compliments.

1 pound ground beef
1 medium onion, chopped
1 clove garlic, chopped
½ teaspoon hot chili powder
½ teaspoon cumin
Dash oregano
1 rounded teaspoon peanut butter
Dash cayenne
Dash cinnamon
Salt to taste
1 can tomatoes
Water
12 tortillas
1½ cups Cheddar cheese, grated

Makes 12.

Combine meat, half of onion and garlic in saucepan and brown. Add next 8 ingredients, and enough water to make soupy. Cook 2 hours on low heat.

After 2 hours, dampen tortillas in sauce to soften. Fill with meat sauce, 1 cup cheese and remaining onion. Roll up and place in 8 × 12-inch baking dish.

Bake at 375° for 30 minutes. Remove from oven. Sprinkle with remaining cheese and return to oven until cheese melts.

SPANAKOPETA (Greek Spinach Pie)

3 bunches fresh spinach
4 tablespoons olive oil
2 bunches scallions or green onions, finely chopped
8 large eggs
½ pound Feta cheese, crumbled
8-ounces cream cheese, softened
8-ounces pot cheese or dry cottage cheese
½ cup parsley, minced
½ teaspoon dried dill
¼ teaspoon white pepper
1 cup butter
1 pound Phyllo pastry leaves

Serves 12.

Wash and dry spinach thoroughly. Trim off stems and chop leaves coarsely. In large frying pan heat olive oil over medium heat. Saute scallions until wilted and soft. Add chopped spinach and saute until moisture evaporates. Set aside to cool.

In a large bowl, beat eggs. Add Feta, cream cheese, pot or cottage cheese, parsley, dill and pepper. Mix well. Add spinach and scallions and mix well.

Melt butter over low heat, without browning. Butter 9 × 13-inch baking pan. Remove Phyllo from package and open carefully. Pastry is paper thin and fragile. Cover pastry not in use with plastic wrap. Removing one sheet at a time, place in baking pan. Carefully brush each sheet with melted butter, using a soft pastry brush. Continue layering sheets and brushing with butter until 10 to 12 sheets are in pan. Be careful not to use too much butter (do not soak pastry). After 10 to 12 sheets are in place, spread spinach/cheese mixture in pan. Cover with 10 more sheets of pastry, brushing each with melted butter. Brush top sheet with butter.

Bake 30 to 40 minutes at 350° or until top is puffed and golden brown.

To serve, cut into squares, small for appetizers or larger, 3 by 3-inches, for side dish.

CHICKEN TURNOVERS

1 3-ounce package cream cheese
1 tablespoon milk
1¼ cups cooked chicken, shredded
1 cup (4 ounces) Cheddar cheese, shredded
1 4-ounce can green chilies
¼ cup green onions, sliced
½ teaspoon garlic salt
½ teaspoon ground cumin
2 cups buttermilk baking mix
½ cup water
3 tablespoons butter, melted
1⅓ cups (about 6-ounces) corn chips, crushed

Serves 6.

Let cream cheese stand at room temperature to soften. Mix with milk, chicken, Cheddar, chilies, onion, garlic salt and cumin. Set aside. Stir baking mix with water until blended. Turn onto a board dusted with baking mix. Knead about 10 times to form ball. Roll out a 12 × 18-inch rectangle. Cut into 6-inch squares. Spoon ⅓ cup of chicken mixture onto each square. Fold squares into triangles and press edges with a fork to seal. Brush with melted butter, then press turnovers into crushed chips to coat. Place on an ungreased cookie sheet. Bake at 400° for 20 minutes or until golden.

CREPES FARCIES NICOISE

Crepe Batter:
1 cup flour
1½ cups milk
3 eggs
Salt and pepper
3 tablespoons butter, melted and cooled

Filling:
1 large eggplant, unpeeled and cubed
2 zucchini, cubed
Salt
¾ cup olive oil
2 medium onions, thinly sliced

Filling (continued):
1 green pepper, thinly sliced
1 red pepper or 1 cup pimento, thinly sliced
4 large ripe tomatoes, seeded, peeled and chopped
1 teaspoon dried basil
½ teaspoon dried oregano
2 tablespoons fresh parsley, chopped
2 cloves garlic, minced
Salt and pepper to taste
12 to 16 slices of thinly sliced cooked ham
¾ cup butter, melted
½ cup Parmesan cheese, grated

Serves 6.

To make crepes, combine the flour, milk, eggs, salt and pepper in a blender. Mix at top speed for 30 seconds and scrape down the sides of jar. Mix again for 30 seconds. Whisk in the butter, pour the batter into a mixing bowl and let stand at room temperature for 1 to 2 hours. Heat a 6-inch crepe pan and brush it lightly with butter. When the pan is very hot, remove it from heat and add 2 tablespoons of batter. Quickly turn the pan in all directions to coat its entire surface. Pour out excess batter. Place the pan over medium heat and cook the crepe until it is lightly browned, then loosen it with the tip of a sharp knife. Lift the edge and quickly turn it with your fingers. Brown lightly on the other side and slide onto plate. Brush pan lightly with butter before making next crepe. Makes 12 to 16 crepes.

To make filling, sprinkle the eggplant and zucchini with salt and let drain, separately, on paper towels for ½ to 1 hour, then dry them thoroughly. Heat ½ cup olive oil in a large, heavy skillet. Add eggplant and saute over high heat until they are browned on all sides. Remove with a slotted spoon to a side dish. Add remaining oil to the pan, then add zucchini, cooking over high heat until they are nicely browned. Remove to side dish. Add the onion, red and green peppers and tomatoes to the skillet. Cook until onions and peppers are soft and all tomato juices have evaporated. Add basil, oregano, parsley, garlic, salt and pepper. Reduce heat, return eggplant and zucchini to pan and cook all for 5 to 6 minutes. Set aside. Line each crepe with the ham, then fill with a heaping tablespoon of vegetable mixture. Roll up the crepes, tucking in ends, and place in a well-buttered baking dish. Dribble melted butter over crepes and sprinkle with cheese. Cover dish and bake for 15 to 20 minutes at 350°. Crepes should be well heated and cheese melted. Serve immediately.

VEGETABLES AND SIDE DISHES

VEGETABLES AND SIDE DISHES

ASPARAGUS PUFFS

A sensational luncheon entree, appetizer or side dish.

24 fresh asparagus spears
¾ cup pimiento-stuffed green olives, finely chopped
4-ounces Swiss cheese, finely chopped
4-ounces cream cheese, room temperature
¼ cup fine dry breadcrumbs
2 egg yolks, room temperature
1 tablespoon fresh lemon juice
¼ teaspoon freshly ground pepper
6 5 by 5-inch squares puff pastry, ⅛-inch thick

Serves 6.

Blanch 6 asparagus spears 2 minutes. Drain and chop finely.

Cook remaining spears just until crisp-tender. Trim to 5-inch lengths.

Grease baking sheet. Combine in a large bowl the blanched asparagus spears with olives, cheeses, breadcrumbs, egg yolks, lemon juice and pepper. Blend well. Divide the mixture into 6 portions. Spread 1 portion over bottom ⅔ of 1 pastry square.

Arrange 3 asparagus spears over filling. Brush top ⅓ of square with water. Roll square up from bottom to top, enclosing asparagus. Place seam side down on prepared baking sheet. Repeat with remaining cheese mixture, pastry squares and asparagus. Cover and refrigerate 1 hour.

Preheat oven to 325°. Bake until pastry is puffed and golden brown, about 20 minutes. Serve immediately.

ASPARAGUS VENETIAN

2-pounds fresh asparagus
1/3 cup melted butter
1 tablespoon onion soup mix
1 cup diced mozarella cheese
2 tablespoons grated Parmesan cheese

Serves 6.

Blanch asparagus in boiling water for 2 minutes; immerse in ice water to cool thoroughly. Drain well. Mix melted butter and onion soup mix. Arrange asparagus in 8-inch baking dish. Drizzle with onion butter. Sprinkle with cheeses. Bake at 450° for 10 minutes.

GOURMET ASPARAGUS

Asparagus is yet another specialty of the Yakima Valley. Grown amongst the orchards, the green spears provide a Spring bonus crop as the orchardist readies the land for fall apple harvest. Last year alone, 96 million pounds were produced by growers.

Olive oil
12 fresh asparagus
1½ cups American cheese, grated
½ cup Romano cheese, grated
1 cup cooked shrimp
2 eggs
1 cup sauterne
1 tablespoon Worcestershire sauce
1 teaspoon cayenne sauce
1½ teaspoons salt
1 can cream of mushroom soup, undiluted
¾ cup bread crumbs

Serves 4.

Coat casserole dish with olive oil and line with asparagus. Layer with half of the required cheeses, add the cooked shrimp and layer the remaining cheeses.

Beat the 2 eggs well, adding the sauterne a little at a time. Blend in Worcestershire sauce, cayenne sauce and salt. Beat again and pour over casserole.

Spread undiluted soup over all and sprinkle bread crumbs on top. Bake at 350° for 45 minutes or until bubbly and brown. Can also be baked covered with foil, according to taste.

PICKLED WASHINGTON ASPARAGUS

For Northwesterners, Spring heralds the coming of asparagus — glorious green stalks, prized since Roman times.

½ cup boiling water
2 to 3 tablespoons sugar
½ teaspoon salt
⅛ teaspoon pepper
½ cup vinegar
2 cups asparagus spears or pieces
1 clove garlic
⅛ teaspoon dill (if desired)

Makes 1 pint.

Combine boiling water, sugar, salt and pepper; stir to dissolve. Add vinegar; chill. Wash asparagus, remove bottom scales. Cut into 1½-inch lengths, if desired. Blanch asparagus in boiling water for 2 minutes; immerse in ice water to cool thoroughly. Drain and pack into pint containers; add garlic clove and dill. Cover with cold pickling solution and refrigerate at least 2 days. Keep refrigerated.

BROCCOLI WITH RED PEPPER HOLLANDAISE

Red peppers add zip to a long-time favorite.

4 egg yolks, room temperature
¼ teaspoon salt
Freshly ground pepper
2 tablespoons freshly squeezed lemon juice
12 tablespoons hot, melted butter
1 red bell pepper, roasted, peeled and pureed or
1 6-ounce jar pimentos, drained and pureed
2-pounds fresh broccoli

Serves 8.

In a blender or food processor, combine egg yolks, salt, pepper and lemon juice. Blend 2 to 3 minutes. With appliance running, pour in hot butter in a steady stream. Add pepper puree and blend. Pour into a non-aluminum bowl. Set in a pan of warm water to keep warm until serving.

Cut broccoli into spears. Steam until tender, about 5 minutes. Pour hollandaise over broccoli; serve immediately.

BRANDIED CARROTS

Brandy transforms ordinary carrots into a celebration.

1-pound carrots
¼ cup butter, melted
¼ cup brandy
1 teaspoon sugar
1 teaspoon salt
Parsley flakes

Serves 6.

Cut the carrots into long, thin strips (approximately the size used for a vegetable tray).

Mix together melted butter, brandy, sugar and salt. Pour the mixture over the carrots. Sprinkle with parsley flakes. Bake in a covered 1½ quart casserole dish for 40 minutes at 375°.

GINGER CANDIED CARROTS

Spicy and sweet — an attractive accompaniment to any entree.

12 medium carrots, peeled and cut into 1-inch lengths
4 tablespoons butter, melted
¼ cup brown sugar
1½ teaspoons ground ginger
½ teaspoon caraway seeds or celery seeds

Serves 4 to 6.

Cover carrots with cold water; cook over medium heat until tender, about 15 to 20 minutes. Melt butter in saucepan. Add brown sugar, ginger and caraway or celery seeds. Drain carrots. Pour butter mixture over carrots. Simmer over low heat for five minutes.

ESCALLOPED ONIONS

Walla Walla onions don't always have to be served raw to showcase their sweet, mild flavor.

4 large Walla Walla sweet onions, sliced
6 slices day-old white or sourdough bread, cubed
1 cup Roquefort cheese, crumbled
1 teaspoon salt
½ teaspoon pepper
1 10-ounce can evaporated milk
3 large eggs, beaten
4 tablespoons butter or margarine

Serves 10 to 12.

Slice onions and parboil for 8 minutes in 2-quart saucepan. Drain onions well.

Butter casserole dish or spray with vegetable coating. Place onions in bottom of pan. Cover onions with cubed bread, then cover with crumbled cheese. Sprinkle with salt and pepper. Mix evaporated milk and eggs together. Pour over onions. Top with pats of butter. Bake at 375° uncovered for 40 to 45 minutes. Serve immediately.

ONION PIE

An easy side dish or appetizer.

1 unbaked pie shell, 8 or 9-inch
½ to ¾ cup cream
2 large onions, thinly sliced
3 tablespoons butter or margarine
1 egg
Salt and pepper to taste
Nutmeg to taste
⅓ cup grated Parmesan cheese

Serves 8.

Pat unbaked pie shell with small amount of cream and chill. Saute onions in butter until transparent.

Bake pie shell at 400° for 2 minutes.

Remove from oven and add onions. Beat egg and ½ cup cream together and pour over onions. Sprinkle top of pie with salt, pepper and nutmeg. Cover with Parmesan cheese.

Bake at 350° for about 30 minutes.

HOMESTEAD CORN PUDDING

Rich and satisfying. . . a dish that spells "home."

4 cups milk
½ cup plus 2 tablespoons yellow cornmeal
¼ cup sugar
½ teaspoon salt
8-ounces fresh yellow corn kernels
4 eggs, well-beaten
½ cup butter, melted
1 teaspoon vanilla
1 teaspoon baking powder

Serves 8.

Grease 2½-quart baking dish. Scald milk in large saucepan. Remove from heat. Stir in cornmeal, sugar and salt. Place over medium-high heat and bring to boil. Reduce heat to medium-low and simmer, stirring constantly, 5 minutes. Remove from heat and stir in corn. Gradually add egg, stirring vigorously. Add butter, vanilla and baking powder and blend well. Turn into prepared dish. Bake at 350° for 45 to 50 minutes or until set. Serve hot.

LEMON PILAF

A superior accompaniment to barbequed salmon — or any fish!

¼ cup butter
1 cup onion, chopped
1 teaspoon garlic, finely minced
2 cups long grain white rice
½ cup fresh lemon juice
¼ cup fresh parsley, minced
1 teaspoon thyme
½ teaspoon basil
½ teaspoon dill weed
½ teaspoon salt
¼ teaspoon pepper
½ cup Parmesan cheese, grated
2¾ cups chicken broth, heated to boiling

Serves 8.

Heat butter over medium heat in Dutch oven. When melted, add the onion and garlic. Stir frequently. After two or three minutes, add the rice, tossing grains well to coat with butter. Saute for a minute or two. Add lemon juice, parsley, seasonings and cheese. Mix well. Add the boiling chicken broth (this is important — cold broth will make the final dish heavier and sticky). Stir well. Cover with lid, and place in a preheated 350° oven. Bake for 20 minutes. The rice should be done. If it's not, add a bit more broth and cook for an additional 5 minutes. Remove from oven and fluff with two forks. Serve in a pretty covered casserole dish. A parsley sprig, dill sprig, or lemon slice would garnish nicely.

POTATOES WITH LEMON CHIVE BUTTER

Boiled to just tender, these red potatoes are a choice companion to any entree.

16 small red potatoes, about 1¾ pounds
3 tablespoons butter or margarine
2 tablespoons chives, chopped
1 tablespoon lemon juice
Salt

Serves 8.

About 25 minutes before serving, wash potatoes. Using a vegetable peeler or knife, peel a strip around the middle of each potato. In a saucepan over high heat, heat potatoes and enough water to cover to boiling. Reduce heat to low, cover. Cook potatoes for 15 minutes or until tender.

Drain potatoes. Return to saucepan. Over low heat, add butter or margarine, chives, lemon juice and salt to taste. Gently toss until potatoes are well-coated. Serve.

POTATOES AU GRATIN

A trust-worthy and always delectable cheese-filled classic.

1½-pounds potatoes, unpeeled
Salt
2 tablespoons butter
2 tablespoons flour
1½ cups hot milk
½ cup sharp cheddar cheese, shredded
¼ cup Parmesan cheese, freshly grated
1 clove garlic, minced
Pepper, freshly ground

Topping:
½ cup sharp cheddar cheese, shredded
¼ cup Parmesan cheese, freshly grated
Paprika

Serves 6 to 8.

Boil potatoes in lightly salted water until tender. Cool, peel and cut into ¼-inch slices. Layer slices in buttered casserole dish.

Melt butter in medium saucepan and stir in flour until mixture is smooth. Gradually add hot milk, stirring constantly. Stir in cheeses and garlic. Continue cooking until cheese is melted. Season to taste with salt and pepper.

Pour sauce over potatoes and sprinkle with cheddar, Parmesan and paprika. Bake for 20 minutes at 350°. Place under broiler just until brown and bubbly. Serve immediately.

TWICE BAKED POTATOES

Eternally popular, this combination can be served as a light entree. Serve with a tart salad.

6 medium baking potatoes
¼ cup margarine or butter
½ to ¾ cup milk
1½ cups sour cream
½ cup Parmesan cheese
10 slices of bacon, cooked and crumbled
½ cup green onions, chopped

Serves 6.

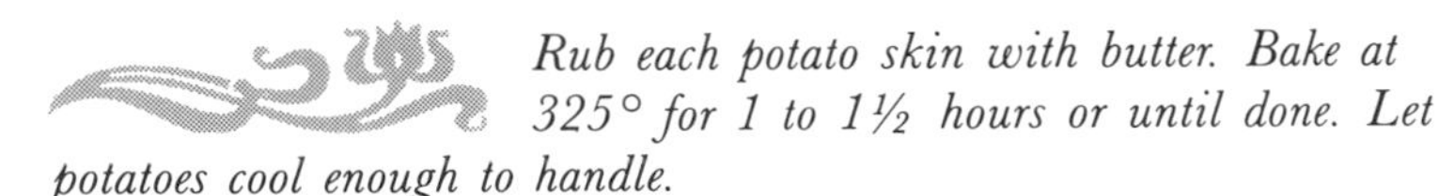

Rub each potato skin with butter. Bake at 325° for 1 to 1½ hours or until done. Let potatoes cool enough to handle.

Cut potatoes lengthwise ⅓ of the way down and all the way through. Scoop the hot potato from both top and bottom into a bowl. Reserve the shells.

Beat 3 tablespoons butter, ½ cup milk, ½ cup sour cream and cheese into the potato until fluffy. Mix in bacon and onions. Fill the bottom part of the reserved shells.

Bake at 425° for 15 minutes or until tops are brown. Pass remaining sour cream for topping.

BLUE CHEESE BACON POTATOES

Blue cheese updates the twice-baked potato.

4 medium baking potatoes
½ cup sour cream
1-ounce blue cheese, crumbled, about ¼ cup
¼ cup milk
4 tablespoons butter or margarine
¾ teaspoon salt
Dash of pepper
4 slices bacon, crisp cooked, drained and crumbled

Serves 4.

Rub potatoes with butter or margarine. Bake in hot oven at 400° for 1 hour or until potatoes are done. Remove from oven. Cut a lengthwise slice from top of each potato. Scoop out inside of each. Mash and add sour cream, blue cheese, milk, butter, salt and pepper. Beat with electric beater until fluffy. Spoon mixture lightly into potato shells. Place on baking sheet. Return to hot oven for 15 minutes or until heated through. Sprinkle with crumbled bacon.

STUFFED HONEY RUM SWEET POTATOES

Baking is the simplest and perhaps best way to cook sweet potatoes.

6 sweet potatoes
¼ cup butter
¼ cup heavy cream
2 tablespoons honey
2 tablespoons dark rum
½ teaspoon ground cardamon
Salt to taste
Pepper to taste
½ cup walnuts, chopped

Serves 6.

Prick potatoes with fork and bake for 25 minutes or until tender at 425°. Cutting lengthwise, slice off top ⅓ of potato. Scrape pulp out of potatoes being careful to keep shell intact. Save bottom portion of shell. Mash pulp and add butter, cream, honey, rum, cardamon, salt and pepper. Beat mixture until fluffy. Return pulp to potato skins. Top with walnuts. Bake for 10 minutes at 450°. To make ahead, refrigerate stuffed potatoes and then bake just before serving.

SPICED CRANBERRIES

Bursting with flavor, use as an accompaniment to turkey or present at holiday time as a gift with your personal touch.

¾ cup water
2 cups sugar
1 tablespoon fresh lemon juice
½ teaspoon allspice
¼ teaspoon cloves
1 teaspoon cinnamon
1-pound fresh cranberries

Makes 1 quart.

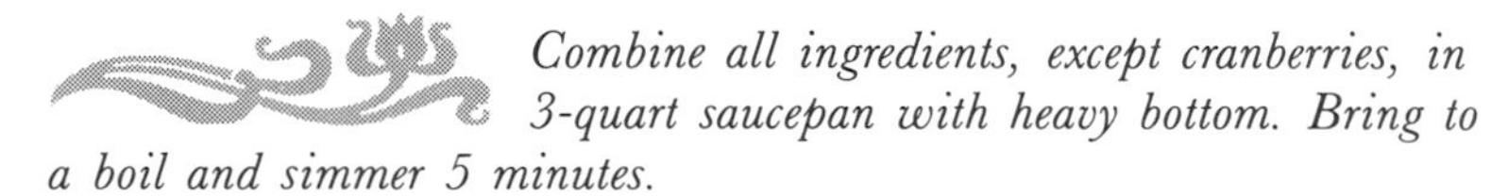

Combine all ingredients, except cranberries, in 3-quart saucepan with heavy bottom. Bring to a boil and simmer 5 minutes.

Add cranberries. Cook over medium-low heat until skins pop open. May be stored in refrigerator in a sealed container for holiday meals or packaged in attractive containers for holiday gifts.

PEACH CHUTNEY

Here's another fine recipe that lends itself to gift-giving.

7-pounds peaches, peeled and chopped
6 red onions, diced
3-pounds sugar
2-pounds raisins
4 cups cider vinegar
1 tablespoon chili powder
1 tablespoon mustard seed
1 tablespoon salt
1 teaspoon curry powder
1 teaspoon tumeric
1 teaspoon cinnamon

Makes 10 pints.

Combine all ingredients in large saucepan. Bring to boil, stirring constantly to keep from burning. Turn down heat and simmer uncovered about 1½ hours or until thick. Ladle into hot, sterilized jars and seal.

APPLES

APPLES

YAKIMA APPLE AND PEAR SALAD

Try adding slices of smoked chicken breast for a substantial main course. Savor the sweet union of two Northwest favorites in this refreshing salad.

Salad:
3 heads Belgium endive
3 cups assorted torn greens
2 cups apples, julienned
2 cups pears, julienned
1 cup Gorgonzola cheese, crumbled
1 cup pecan halves, roasted

Orange Vinaigrette Dressing:
1 cup olive oil
1 cup walnut oil
1 cup tarragon vinegar
2 tablespoons frozen orange juice, thawed
Salt to taste
Pepper, freshly ground, to taste

Serves 6 to 8.

Place 3 to 4 spears of washed and drained Belgium endive in a sunburst pattern on a chilled salad plate. Place washed and drained torn salad greens on the Belgium endive spears. Casually arrange the julienne of apples and pears on the torn greens. Sprinkle lightly with crumbles of Gorgonzola cheese and roasted pecan halves. Combine dressing ingredients. Spoon the dressing over the salad to taste.

DOUBLE DELICIOUS SALAD PLATE WITH APPLE-DILL DRESSING

This "double delicious" recipe presents a sampling of the Northwest's famous bounty. Healthful vegetables, world-class salmon and, of course, apples from the "Apple Capital of the World," all combine for an authentic taste of the Northwest's finest.

Salad:
1½-pounds broccoli spears
2-pounds asparagus spears
1½-pounds carrots, peeled and cut into julienne strips
2 to 3-pounds poached salmon
12 large Red or Golden Delicious apples, cored and sliced
1½-pounds lettuce leaves
1½-pounds cherry tomatoes, if desired

Dressing:
1½ large Golden Delicious apple, cored
3 tablespoons lime juice
1 clove garlic
½ cup mayonnaise or salad dressing
4-ounces cream cheese
½ tablespoon chives, chopped
¼ teaspoon dill weed
½ teaspoon onion powder
¾ cups walnuts, toasted and chopped, optional

Serves 12.

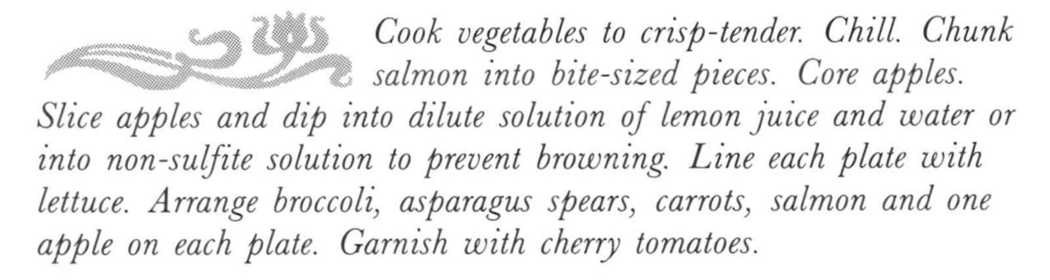

Cook vegetables to crisp-tender. Chill. Chunk salmon into bite-sized pieces. Core apples. Slice apples and dip into dilute solution of lemon juice and water or into non-sulfite solution to prevent browning. Line each plate with lettuce. Arrange broccoli, asparagus spears, carrots, salmon and one apple on each plate. Garnish with cherry tomatoes.

To make dressing, place the remaining ingredients in food processor or blender. Blend dressing until fairly smooth.

Serve each salad with approximately ⅓ cup dressing.

APPLE-CRAB SALAD

This crunchy, nutty salad makes an unusual luncheon main dish.

1-pound fresh crab meat
1 large Red Delicious apple, sliced thinly
1 cup whole pecans
1 cup red seedless grapes
Gargonzola cheese, crumbled
1 cup sour cream
¾ cup mayonnaise

Serves 6 to 8.

Combine first five ingredients. Combine sour cream and mayonnaise. Stir crab mixture into dressing mixture. Chill at least 2 hours before serving. Serve on a bed of red leaf lettuce and garnish with a thin slice of lemon and a sprig of parsley.

WASHINGTON DELICIOUS APPLE LAYERED SALAD

Salad:
3 cups Red or Golden Delicious apples, cored and diced
1 tablespoon lime juice
1 cup celery, diced
1 orange, pared, sliced and halved
1 cup seedless green grapes, halved
½ cup pecans, chopped

Creamy Dressing:
⅓ cup mayonnaise
⅓ cup sour cream
2 tablespoons blue cheese, crumbled

Garnish:
Blue cheese
Apple slices

Serves 6.

Toss diced apples with lime juice. Place half in bottom of 3-inch deep 2-quart glass bowl. Layer celery, orange, grapes, pecans and remaining apples in bowl.

To make dressing, combine ingredients. Mix well.

Spread dressing over salad. Garnish with blue cheese and apple slices.

APPLE FRUIT SALAD

A delicacy with any light meal — especially brunch.

Salad:
1 Red Delicious apple, cored and wedged
1 Golden Delicious apple, cored and wedged
1 orange, peeled and sliced
2 kiwi, peeled and sliced
Lettuce

Dressing:
2 tablespoons honey
2 tablespoons vegetable oil
¼ teaspoon salt
Generous dash of cayenne pepper
2 tablespoons lime juice

Serves 6.

Arrange all fruit on lettuce lined platters. Combine dressing ingredients. Lightly pour spicy lime dressing over fruit. Use extra dressing for dipping.

HARVEST BISQUE

This soup is a delightful cornucopia of Autumn flavors.

1 onion, chopped
2 leeks, including 2-inches of green tops, washed well and chopped
½ cup celery, chopped
1 stick plus 1 tablespoon unsalted butter
½ cup carrot, chopped
1-pound butternut squash, peeled, seeded and chopped
1 small turnip, peeled and chopped
2 large tart cooking apples, peeled, cored and chopped
4 cups chicken stock or chicken broth
6 tablespoons flour
1 cup unpasteurized apple cider
¼ teaspoon fresh nutmeg, grated
¼ teaspoon dried rosemary, crumbled
¼ teaspoon dried sage, crumbled
Salt and pepper to taste
½ cup heavy cream
½ cup Gruyére, grated
Croutons for garnish, if desired

Serves 6 to 8.

In a kettle cook the onion, leeks and celery in 3 tablespoons of the butter over moderate heat, stirring for 5 minutes or until softened. Add the carrot, squash, turnip, apples and the stock. Bring the stock to a boil and simmer the mixture for 45 minutes or until the vegetables are soft.

In a small saucepan melt remaining 6 tablespoons butter over moderate heat. Add the flour and cook the roux, stirring for 3 minutes. Remove the pan from the heat and add 1 cup of the liquid from the soup mixture in a stream while stirring. Stir the mixture into the remaining soup mixture. Add the cider, nutmeg, rosemary, sage and salt and pepper to taste and simmer the soup for 10 minutes. Stir in the cream and the Gruyére, ladle the soup into heated bowls and garnish it with the croutons if desired.

HERBED APPLE AND WILD RICE DRESSING

Festive enough for formal dinners, this dressing is certain to become a part of your family's meal-time tradition.

½ cup onion, chopped
2 tablespoons vegetable oil
1 cup white rice, uncooked
1 cup wild rice, uncooked
4 cups hot water
¾ teaspoon salt
½ teaspoon thyme, crushed
½ teaspoon oregano, crushed
¼ teaspoon pepper
3 cups Golden Delicious apples, cored, peeled and chopped
½ cup pecans, coarsely chopped or hazelnuts, coarsely chopped
¼ cup parsley, chopped

Serves 8 to 10.

Saute onion in oil until tender. Add white rice and wild rice. Cook and stir until coated with oil. Add water, salt, thyme, oregano and pepper. Bring to a boil. Reduce heat and simmer covered for 30 minutes. Add apples, nuts and parsley. Continue to simmer or bake in 3-quart covered baking dish at 375° for 15 to 30 minutes or until liquid is absorbed and wild rice is tender. Makes enough stuffing for a 12-pound turkey or halve recipe for a roasting chicken.

APPLE-SAUSAGE STUFFED ACORN SQUASH

2 1-pound acorn squash
12-ounces bulk pork sausage
¼ cup onion, chopped
1½ cups Golden Delicious Apples, cored and chopped
¼ teaspoon sage, crushed
¼ teaspoon thyme, crushed
⅛ teaspoon pepper
Dash of salt
Almonds, blanched and slivered, optional

Serves 8.

Halve squash. Remove seeds. Place cut side down in baking dish. Bake for 30 minutes at 350°.

Sauté sausage and onion until browned and crumbly. Drain excess fat. Add apples and seasonings. Sauté 5 minutes longer.

Turn squash cut-side up, fill cavities with apple and sausage mixture. Sprinkle with almonds. Cover with foil. Bake for 20 to 30 minutes at 350° until squash is tender.

APPLE BEANS

This hearty side dish — perfect for picnics or outdoor gatherings — comes highly recommended.

2 15-ounce cans dark red kidney beans, drained
3 16-ounce cans pork and beans
1 15-ounce can diced tomatoes in a rich puree
2-pounds bulk pork sausage, browned and drained, reserving drippings
1 Walla Walla onion, chopped and sauteed in 2 tablespoons of sausage drippings
2 cloves garlic
1 cup brown sugar, packed
2 Red Delicious apples, shredded
1 teaspoon chili powder
1 teaspoon salt

Serves 6 to 8.

Combine all ingredients in a covered dish. Bake for 2 hours at 350°.

CINNAMON-APPLE DUTCH BABY

Bring old-fashioned goodness into your kitchen with the inviting aroma of apples and cinnamon.

6 tablespoons butter or margarine
2 teaspoons ground cinnamon
¼ cup sugar
2 large Gravenstein, Granny Smith or green Golden Delicious apples, peeled and cored
4 eggs
1 cup flour
1 cup milk
Powdered sugar

Serves 6.

In a 10 to 12-inch frying pan, melt butter over medium-high heat. Stir in cinnamon and sugar. Thinly slice apples into pan. Cook, stirring until apples are translucent, about 5 minutes.

Either place pan uncovered in a 425° oven while you mix batter or transfer apples to a glass ovenproof dish, 10-inch rectangle or round, and keep in oven.

In a blender or food processor, whirl eggs and flour until smooth. Blend in milk. Pour batter evenly over apples in pan. Bake uncovered until pancake is puffy and golden, about 15 minutes.

Dust with powdered sugar and let stand 5 minutes. Cut into wedges and serve immediately.

NORMANDY FRENCH TOAST

Custard Sauce:
1 large apple, cored
1 tablespoon butter
1 tablespoon vegetable oil
¾ cup light cream
2 egg yolks
¼ cup sugar
1 teaspoon flour
½ teaspoon vanilla
2 tablespoons rum

French Toast:
1 baguette of French bread
2 eggs
2 tablespoons sugar
2 cups milk
1 teaspoon vanilla
¼ teaspoon salt
¼ cup rum
Butter
Vegetable oil

Serves 5 to 10.

To prepare sauce, slice 10 very thin rings from the thickest portion of apple. Peel and dice remaining apple. Sauté apple rings and dice apple in butter and oil until just softened and set aside. Scald cream. Beat egg yolks, sugar and flour until smooth and place in a saucepan. Add cream slowly to egg mixture, stirring constantly. Add vanilla and cook until thickened. Add rum and diced apples.

To prepare French toast, slice bread diagonally into 10 1-inch thick pieces. Make batter by combining the eggs, sugar, milk, vanilla, salt and rum. Dip bread into batter and sauté both sides in butter-oil mixture until golden brown. Remove from pan and cover each piece with 2 to 3 tablespoons of custard sauce and top with an apple ring.

Both sauce and toast may be prepared in advance. Reheat the French toast on a cookie sheet at 350° for 15 minutes. Add warmed sauce, top with apple rings and heat 5 minutes more.

APPLE AND CHEESE ROLLS

This Washington State Apple Commission favorite complements soup or salad.

2 cups apples, peeled, cored and chopped
2 tablespoons onion, chopped
2 tablespoons butter or margarine
2 teaspoons lemon juice
½ teaspoon oregano, crushed
½ teaspoon lemon peel, grated
¼ teaspoon pepper
4-ounces Mozzarella cheese, shredded
1 14 to 16-ounce loaf frozen yeast bread dough, thawed

Makes 30 rolls.

Preheat oven to 350°F.

Sauté apples and onion in butter until barely tender. Stir in lemon juice, oregano, lemon peel, and pepper. Cool slightly; stir in cheese.

Roll dough to 15 by 8-inch rectangle. Spread apple cheese mixture over dough, leaving about 1-inch uncovered on one lengthwise edge.

Tightly roll dough in a jelly roll fashion from lengthwise edge; moisten edge with water and seal.

Cut into ½-inch slices. Place on greased baking sheet about 1½-inches apart. Cover and let rise until doubled in size.

Bake for 25 to 30 minutes or until lightly browned. Serve warm.

APPLE RING

Dough:
¾ cup lukewarm milk
¼ cup sugar
1 teaspoon salt
1 envelope dry yeast
¼ cup lukewarm water
1 egg, slightly beaten
¼ cup butter, softened
3½ cups sifted flour
2 tablespoons butter, melted

Filling:
¾ cup cooked dried prunes, cut up
1½ cups Golden Delicious apples, cored, peeled and diced
1 tablespoon lemon juice
½ cup brown sugar
1 teaspoon cinnamon
¾ cup walnuts, chopped

Powdered Sugar Glaze:
½ cup powdered sugar
1 tablespoon milk
¼ teaspoon vanilla

Serves 8.

To prepare dough, combine the milk, sugar and salt in a bowl. Dissolve the yeast in lukewarm water (105° to 115°F.). Add the dissolved yeast to the milk mixture and stir. Add the egg and ¼ cup butter. Stir in just enough flour to make the dough easy to handle.

Turn out the dough on a lightly floured board and knead until smooth and elastic, about 5 to 10 minutes.

Place in a greased bowl, turning once to bring greased side up. Cover and let rise in a warm spot until double in bulk, 1½ to 2 hours. Punch down; let rise again until double, 30 to 45 minutes.

Roll the dough into a 9 by 18-inch oblong. Spread with melted butter.

To prepare filling, combine the prunes, apples, lemon juice, brown sugar, cinnamon and walnuts. Spread over the dough. Roll up from the long side, seal edge and form into a circle, sealed edge down, on a lightly greased baking sheet. Seal the ends together.

Bake ring at 350° for 45 minutes. Mix glaze ingredients. Frost when cool.

GOLDEN APPLE TORTE

Serve warm or cooled with whipped cream or ice cream. Decorate with a sprig of holly and voilá, a beautiful Christmas gift.

Dough:
2 cups flour
½ cup sugar
2 teaspoons baking powder
Dash salt
½ cup butter, softened
1 egg
2 tablespoons cold water

Filling:
6 cups Golden Delicious apples, peeled and cored
4 teaspoons lemon juice
¼ cup raisins
⅓ cup sugar
2 tablespoons flour
1 teaspoon cinnamon
1 tablespoon butter
¼ cup milk
1 egg yolk, beaten

Serves 12.

To prepare dough, combine flour, sugar, baking powder and salt. Blend in butter, egg and water. Chill ⅓ of dough. Pat remaining ⅔ of dough on bottom and halfway up sides of springform pan. Bake at 400° for 10 minutes.

To prepare filling, toss apples with lemon juice and raisins. Mix sugar with flour and cinnamon. Toss with apples and turn into prepared crust. Dot with butter. Roll out chilled dough between 2 pieces of wax paper. Cut into ½-inch strips. Place lattice top over apples. Seal to the edge of the baked pastry. Combine milk and egg yolk. Brush lattice. Bake at 350° for 50 to 60 minutes or until crust is golden brown and apples are tender. Let cool and remove from pan.

BAVARIAN APPLE TORTE

This elegant torte doubles as an after-dinner dessert or as a coffee cake for breakfast or brunch.

Dough:
½ cup butter
⅓ cup sugar
¼ teaspoon vanilla
1 cup flour

Filling:
8-ounces cream cheese, softened
¼ cup sugar
1 egg
½ teaspoon vanilla
4 cups apples, thinly sliced
⅓ cup sugar
½ teaspoon cinnamon
¼ cup almonds, sliced

Serves 8.

To make dough, cream butter and sugar until light and fluffy. Blend in vanilla. Add flour and mix well. Spread dough on bottom and 1½-inches up sides of 9-inch springform pan.

To make filling, combine softened cream cheese and ¼ cup sugar. Blend in egg and vanilla. Pour into pastry lined pan.

Toss apples with ⅓ cup sugar and cinnamon. Spoon apple mixture over cream cheese layer. Sprinkle with nuts.

Bake at 450° for 10 minutes. Reduce oven temperature to 400°. Bake for 25 more minutes. Remove from oven and loosen rim of springform pan. Cool. Remove rim. Chill.

GLAZED FRESH APPLE CAKE

Cake:
2 cups sugar
1½ cups oil
3 eggs
3 cups flour
2 teaspoons cinnamon
1 teaspoon baking soda
½ teaspoon nutmeg
½ teaspoon salt
2 teaspoons vanilla
3 cups apples, pared, cored and diced
Juice of one lemon
1 cup walnuts, chopped

Caramel Glaze:
6 tablespoons butter or margarine
6 tablespoons brown sugar
4 tablespoons heavy cream
1 teaspoon vanilla

Serves 12.

In large bowl, beat sugar and oil until well mixed. Add eggs, one at a time, beating well after each addition. Sift flour, cinnamon, baking soda, nutmeg and salt; add to egg mixture gradually, beating constantly. Add vanilla and combine thoroughly. Sprinkle apples with lemon juice and fold into batter with walnuts. Spoon into well-greased and floured bundt pan or large tube pan. Bake at 325° for 75 minutes or until done. Remove from oven. Cool in pan on wire rack for 15 minutes. Invert onto serving plate and cool completely on wire rack. After completely cooled, glaze.

To prepare glaze, melt butter or margarine in a small saucepan. Add brown sugar, cream and vanilla. Bring to a rolling boil and boil rapidly about 2 minutes or until mixture sheets off a spoon. Cool slightly and spoon over cake so that glaze runs down the sides. Makes about ½ cup of glaze.

Wrap any leftover cake tightly in plastic wrap. It will keep unrefrigerated up to two weeks.

GOLDEN APPLE MERINGUE TART

Pastry:
1 cup flour
2 tablespoons sugar
⅓ cup butter, softened
1 egg yolk, beaten
¼ teaspoon vanilla
1 teaspoon milk

Filling:
3 to 4 Golden Delicious apples, pared, cored and sliced
¼ cup water
1 tablespoon sugar
2 teaspoons cornstarch
¾ teaspoon ground cinnamon
Dash of salt

Topping:
3 egg whites
¼ teaspoon cream of tartar
¼ cup sugar

Makes one 9-inch tart.

Preheat oven to 400°.

To make pastry, combine the flour and sugar. Cut in the softened butter. Stir in the beaten egg yolk and vanilla and mix well. If the mixture is too dry, add milk. Press in the bottom and 1-inch up the sides of a 9-inch springform pan. Bake 8 to 10 minutes. (Pastry may also be pressed onto the bottom and sides of a 9-inch flan pan with removable bottom.) Leave oven at 400°.

To prepare filling, combine the apples and water in a saucepan. Simmer, covered, 5 minutes or until apples are tender. Combine the sugar, cornstarch, cinnamon and salt and stir into the apples. Cook and stir until thickened. Turn mixture into the baked pastry crust.

To prepare topping, beat the egg whites with the cream of tartar until foamy. Gradually add the sugar and beat until stiff peaks form and sugar is dissolved. Spoon the meringue over the apples, sealing to the edges of the pastry.

Bake 5 to 7 minutes or until lightly browned. Serve warm or cool.

CORSICAN CARAMELIZED APPLE TART

1 cup plus 2 tablespoons all-purpose flour
1½ teaspoons baking powder
1¾ cups plus 2 tablespoons sugar
1 teaspoon vanilla
1 teaspoon sugar
6 eggs
2½-pounds Golden Delicious apples, peeled, cored and roughly chopped

Serves 6 to 8.

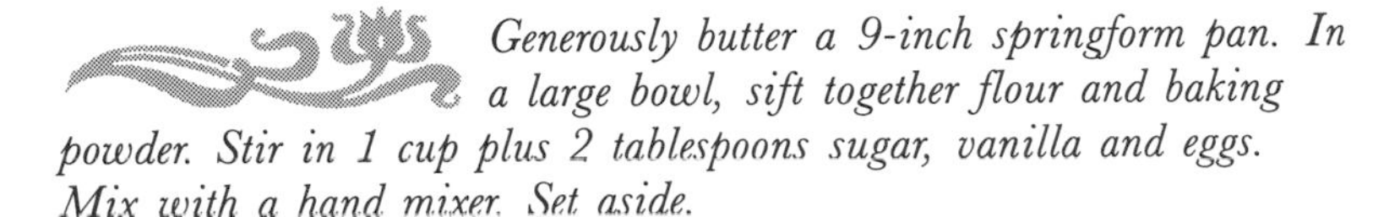

Generously butter a 9-inch springform pan. In a large bowl, sift together flour and baking powder. Stir in 1 cup plus 2 tablespoons sugar, vanilla and eggs. Mix with a hand mixer. Set aside.

In a small bowl dissolve remaining sugar in ¼ cup water and cook, without stirring, until mixture is golden caramel.

Pour the hot caramel into the bottom of the pan, cover caramel with the chopped apples and then pour the batter on top.

Bake at 375° for 45 minutes or until tester comes out clean. While tart is still warm, invert pan onto plate and carefully release pan. Serve at room temperature.

TARTE TATIN

Paté Brisee:
1½ cups flour
¼ teaspoon salt
6 tablespoons unsalted butter
3 tablespoons shortening, chilled
4 to 5 tablespoons ice water

Caramel:
⅓ cup sugar
¼ cup water

Apple Layer:
8 large Golden Delicious or Criterion apples
4 tablespoons butter
⅓ cup sugar
1 tablespoon lemon juice
Rind of 1 lemon, finely grated
Pinch of salt

Egg Wash:
1 whole egg or 1 egg yolk
1 tablespoon water

Serves 8 to 10.

To prepare Paté Brisee, combine flour and salt and cut in butter and shortening. Lightly mix in enough ice water to make a dough that sticks together. Refrigerate. Note: this can be done using food processor.

To prepare caramel, mix sugar and water together in a small saucepan. Boil until they form a straw-colored syrup. Pour into a pie pan and quickly tilt to coat the bottom and partially up the sides.

To prepare apple layer, peel, core and quarter apples. Vertically slice each quarter into thirds. In a large skillet, melt the butter, add sugar, lemon juice, rind and salt. Add the apples and cook over medium heat. Simmer 8 to 10 minutes. Apples should be partially cooked. Remove slices with a slotted spoon to cool on a large, flat surface. Make a decorative, overlapping, circular pattern with the apples on the caramel. Fill with the remaining apple slices.

To make crust, roll the Paté Brisee into a 10-inch circle and lay it over the apples, reaching just to the edge. Brush with egg and water wash. Prick in several places and bake at 400° for 45 minutes or until crust is browned. Let rest 10 minutes. Cover with a serving plate and invert pan. Serve warm or at room temperature.

SPECIAL APPLE PIE

Crust:
1¾ cups all-purpose flour
¼ cup sugar
1 teaspoon cinnamon
½ teaspoon salt
½ cup plus 2 tablespoons butter
¼ cup water or apple cider

Filling:
8 McIntosh apples, peeled, cored and sliced
1⅔ cups sour cream
1 cup sugar
⅓ cup all-purpose flour
1 egg
2 teaspoons vanilla
½ teaspoon salt

Topping:
1 cup walnuts, chopped
½ cup all-purpose flour
⅓ cup brown sugar, firmly packed
⅓ cup sugar
1 tablespoon cinnamon
Pinch of salt
½ cup butter, room temperature

Makes 1 10-inch pie.

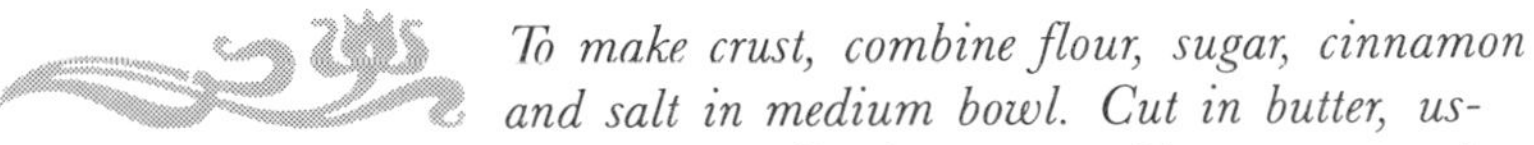

To make crust, combine flour, sugar, cinnamon and salt in medium bowl. Cut in butter, using pastry blender or two knives until mixture resembles coarse meal. Add water and toss mixture gently with fork until evenly moistened. Gather gently into ball. Transfer to lightly floured board and roll into circle slightly larger than a deep 10-inch pie plate. Ease pastry into pan and flute a high edge. Set aside.

For filling, combine all ingredients in large bowl and mix well. Spoon into crust. Bake for 10 minutes at 450°. Reduce oven to 350° and continue baking until filling is slightly puffed and golden brown or about 40 minutes. Cover edges of crust with strips of aluminum foil if it is browning too quickly.

To make topping, combine walnuts, flour, sugars, cinnamon and salt in medium bowl and mix well. Blend in butter until mixture is crumbly. Spoon over pie and bake 15 minutes longer.

FRESH APPLE MOUSSE

4 Jonathan or Winesap apples
½ cup sugar
½ cup water
½ teaspoon vanilla extract
½ pint whipping cream
1 tablespoon sugar
1 teaspoon vanilla extract
1 cup peanut brittle, crushed

Makes 6 to 8 servings.

Pare and core apples. Cut into ¼-inch slices. Combine sugar, water and ½ teaspoon vanilla in pan. Bring to a slow boil. Add apple slices and simmer 5 minutes. Remove from syrup. Cool. Whip cream, add sugar and vanilla. Fold apple slices into whipped cream carefully. In a glass serving bowl, place half the apple and cream mixture and sprinkle generously with crushed peanut brittle. Repeat the layers. Chill several hours before serving.

APLETS

Washington's favorite confection — a true taste of the Northwest.

2-pounds unpeeled McIntosh apples including cores, chopped
1¾ cups sugar
1 tablespoon unflavored gelatin
3 to 4 tablespoons fresh lemon juice or to taste
¾ cup walnuts, chopped
½ cup powdered sugar sifted with 1 tablespoon cornstarch

Makes 32 aplets.

In a heavy 2-quart stainless steel or enameled saucepan combine apples and ¼ cup water. Cook mixture uncovered over moderately low heat, stirring occasionally, for 20 to 30 minutes or until apples are soft. Puree the mixture through the fine disk of a food mill into another heavy stainless steel or enameled saucepan. Add the sugar and cook over moderately low heat, stirring frequently and being careful not to let it burn, for 30 to 40 minutes or until thickened.

In a small bowl sprinkle the gelatin over ¼ cup cold water and let it soften for 15 minutes. Add the gelatin mixture to the apple mixture and heat over low heat stirring until the gelatin is dissolved, but do not let boil. Remove the pan from heat and stir in lemon juice and walnuts. Pour the mixture into an 8-inch square glass baking dish, rinsed with cold water but not dried, and spread it evenly. Let the candy stand uncovered at room temperature for 24 hours. Cut the candy into 2 by 1-inch rectangles and dredge the aplets in powdered sugar mixture, shaking off the excess. Transfer the aplets as they are dredged to a rack and let them dry for at least 8 hours or overnight. Store the aplets in an airtight container lined with wax paper, separating the layers with wax paper.

YAKIMA APPLE BUTTER

Mouth-watering apple butter — simmering aromatically on the stove — is a Northwest Autumn tradition.

8-pounds of tart apples
8 cups apple cider
4 cups sugar
2 teaspoons cinnamon
½ teaspoon nutmeg
¼ teaspoon allspice
⅛ teaspoon cloves

Makes 4 quarts.

Wash, quarter and core apples. Do not pare. Add apples to Dutch oven and add apple cider. Bring apple mixture to a gentle boil and simmer until apples are very soft, about 20 minutes. Strain to remove skins. Return apple pulp to pan and stir in remaining ingredients. Simmer for 2 hours, uncovered, or until mixture is richly brown and very thick. Preserve in hot sterilized jars according to manufacturer's directions.

APPLE SQUARES

An easy-to-pack lunch box treat.

2 cups sifted flour
2 teaspoons baking powder
½ teaspoon salt
½ teaspoon cinnamon
½ cup butter or margarine
1 cup brown sugar, firmly packed
1 cup sugar
2 eggs
2 teaspoons vanilla
1 cup apples, chopped
1 cup nuts, finely chopped
2 tablespoons sugar
½ teaspoon cinnamon

Serves 12.

Sift flour, baking powder, salt and cinnamon onto waxed paper.

Melt butter in saucepan over medium heat. Remove from heat. Beat in sugars, eggs and vanilla with a wooden spoon until smooth.

Stir butter and flour mixtures, apples and nuts, until combined. Spread into a greased 10-inch by 18-inch pan. Sprinkle with remaining sugar mixed with cinnamon. Bake for 30 minutes at 350°. Cool completely. Cut into squares.

DESSERTS

DESSERTS

HEAVENLY CHOCOLATE BERRY PIE

1¼ cups graham cracker crumbs
3 tablespoons sugar
⅓ cup butter or margarine, melted
½ cup plus 2 tablespoons semi-sweet chocolate chips, divided
1 8-ounce package cream cheese, softened
¼ cup brown sugar, firmly packed
½ teaspoon vanilla extract
1 cup whipping cream, whipped
1 pint fresh strawberries
1 teaspoon shortening

Serves 6 to 8.

Combine first three ingredients, mixing well. Firmly press onto bottom and sides of a lightly greased 9-inch pie plate. Bake at 325° for 10 minutes. Cool completely.

Place ½ cup chocolate chips in top of a double boiler. Bring water to a boil. Reduce heat to low. Cook until chocolate melts. Set aside to cool slightly.

Beat cream cheese with an electric mixer until light and fluffy. Add brown sugar and vanilla, mixing well. Add cooled chocolate, mixing well. Fold the whipped cream into cream cheese mixture. Spoon filling into prepared crust. Chill at least 8 hours.

Set aside 1 strawberry. Cut remaining strawberries into thick slices lengthwise. Arrange slices over filling beginning at outer edge and overlapping them while working toward the center. Place the whole strawberry in the center of the pie.

Combine remaining 2 tablespoons chocolate chips and shortening in a small saucepan over low heat. Cook until the chocolate chips melt. Drizzle over strawberries. Keep chilled until ready to serve.

CHERRY CRANBERRY PIE

Crust:
3 cups all-purpose flour
½ cup well-chilled butter, cut into small pieces
6 tablespoons vegetable shortening
½ teaspoon salt
2 egg yolks
5 to 6 tablespoons cold water

Filling:
1 12-ounce bag fresh or frozen cranberries
¾ cup brown sugar, firmly packed
½ teaspoon cinnamon
⅛ teaspoon ground cloves
3 cups frozen pitted cherries, thawed and well-drained with juice reserved
2 tablespoons cornstarch
2 tablespoons cold water
1½ to 2 teaspoons fresh lemon juice
1 teaspoon almond extract
1 egg mixed with 1 tablespoon water
1 tablespoon butter, cut into small pieces

Serves 6 to 8.

To make crust, combine flour, butter, shortening and salt in large bowl and blend until mixture resembles coarse crumbs. Mix in yolks and 3 tablespoons water. Add remaining water a few drops at a time just until dough holds together, do not overmix. Divide dough in half. Form into 2 balls, then flatten into discs. Wrap dough in plastic. Refrigerate while preparing filling.

For filling, combine cranberries, brown sugar and spices in 2-quart saucepan. Add ⅓ cup reserved cherry juice (and water if necessary to make ⅓ cup). Cover and cook over medium heat until ⅔ of cranberries have popped, about 15 minutes. Blend cornstarch and 2 tablespoons water until smooth. Add to cranberry mixture with cherries and cook until thickened, 3 to 5 minutes. Remove from heat. Stir in lemon juice and almond extract. Let cool.

To assemble, grease 9-inch fluted quiche pan or pie plate. Roll half of pastry out on lightly floured surface into 12-inch circle. Fit into prepared pan. Roll remaining pastry out on lightly floured surface into 12-inch circle. Brush with beaten egg mixture to glaze. Cut into ½-inch-wide strips with knife or fluted pastry wheel. Turn filling into crust. Dot with butter. Arrange pastry strips in lattice pattern atop pie, pressing ends into edge of bottom crust. Flute edge of bottom crust decoratively. Bake at 400° until crust is browned and fruit is bubbly, about 25 minutes. Serve pie warm or at room temperature.

RHUBARB MERINGUE PIE

Never Fail Pie Crust:
4 cups flour
1 teaspoon baking powder
2 teaspoons salt
1 tablespoon sugar
1¾ cups shortening
½ cup water
1 beaten egg
1 tablespoon white vinegar or lemon juice

Rhubarb Filling:
3 egg yolks, reserve whites
½ cup honey
¾ cup sugar
2 tablespoons cornstarch
½ 6½-ounce can condensed evaporated milk
1 teaspoon cinnamon
1 to 2 cups rhubarb, chopped

Meringue:
3 egg whites
3 tablespoons sugar
¼ teaspoon cream of tartar
Dash of salt

Serves 6 to 8.

Prepare 1 pie crust using your favorite recipe or try this recipe which makes 4 single pie crusts. Combine dry ingredients. Add wet ingredients. Mix using pastry cutter until dough is thoroughly mixed and forms beads. Mold dough into 4 balls. Roll using floured surface. Place in ungreased pie pans.

To prepare rhubarb filling, combine dry ingredients. Mix egg yolks, honey and milk together. Pour into dry ingredients and add rhubarb. Pour into pie crust. Bake at 350° for 45 minutes.

To make meringue, mix ingredients using electric mixer until egg whites are stiff. Pour onto baked pie. Brown lighlty in oven.

LIME AND SOUR CREAM PIE

¾ cup sugar
3 tablespoons cornstarch
2½ teaspoons freshly grated peel of 2 large limes
⅓ cup fresh lime juice
1 cup half-and-half
¼ cup unsalted butter, room temperature
1 baked 9-inch pie shell
1 cup whipping cream
1 to 2 tablespoons sugar

Serves 6 to 8.

Combine ¾ cup sugar with cornstarch and lime peel in medium saucepan and mix well. Add lime juice and stir until smooth. Blend in half-and-half and butter. Place over medium heat and stir until mixture thickens and starts to boil, about 10 to 12 minutes. Remove from heat and let cool, stirring occasionally. Fold in sour cream. Turn mixture into baked pie shell.

Combine whipping cream and 1 to 2 tablespoons sugar in medium bowl and whip to soft peaks. Spread atop pie and serve.

SAWDUST PIE

1½ cups sugar
1½ cups flaked coconut
1½ cups pecans, chopped
1½ cups graham cracker crumbs
7 egg whites, unbeaten
1 unbaked 10-inch pie shell
Unsweetened whipped cream
1 large banana, thinly sliced

Serves 8 to 10.

Combine sugar, coconut, pecans, graham cracker crumbs and whites in large bowl and mix well. Do not beat. Turn into pie shell. Bake at 350° until filling is just set, about 35 minutes. Do not overbake. Serve warm or at room temperature. Top each serving with generous dollop of whipped cream and several banana slices.

CHOCOLATE PEPPERMINT ICE CREAM PIE

1½ cups chocolate cookie wafers, crushed
6 tablespoons melted butter
1½ tablespoons sugar
1 quart peppermint ice cream, preferably pink
3 egg whites, at room temperature
1 cup marshmallow cream
1 teaspoon vanilla
8-ounces bittersweet or semi-sweet chocolate, melted

Serves 8.

In a 9-inch pie pan, blend crushed wafers, butter and sugar. Press into bottom and up sides. Bake at 350° for 10 minutes. Cool completely. Soften ice cream in refrigerator for 30 minutes. Spoon into crust and smooth top. Wrap airtight. Freeze until hard or at least 12 hours. Pie may be wrapped and stored at this point.

Beat egg whites until stiff. Beat in marshmallow cream one spoonful at a time. Beat until whites hold a peak and curl. Stir in vanilla. Spoon over ice cream, being sure to cover it completely to the crust. Bake at 450° for 2 to 3 minutes until meringue is golden. Wrap airtight and freeze. Pie can be frozen for a few days at this point. To serve, let stand at room temperature for 15 minutes. Cut into wedges and serve with hot, melted chocolate.

MACADEMIA CREAM CRUNCH PIE

9-inch pie shell, baked and cooled

Macadamia Crunch Candy:
¾ cup salted Macademia nuts
¼ teaspoon baking soda
½ cup sugar
¼ cup water
2 tablespoons butter

Filling:
1 envelope unflavored gelatin
¼ cup cold water
3 eggs, separated
½ cup sugar, divided
1 tablespoon rum
1 teaspoon vanilla
1 cup whipping cream

Serves 8.

To make candy, mix nuts and soda together and set aside. Stir ½ cup sugar, ¼ cup water and butter together in a small saucepan. Boil over high heat, stirring until temperature reaches 280° on candy thermometer or just below hard crack stage. Add nut mixture. Remove immediately from heat. Stir until just blended. Pour at once onto a buttered baking sheet. Spread with spoon. Let cool. Crush candy coarsely and store airtight until ready for use.

To make filling, mix gelatin with water and let stand about 5 minutes or until softened; dissolve over hot water. Beat egg whites until stiff, then gradually beat in ¼ cup sugar until whites hold sharp peaks. With same beater, whip egg yolks with remaining ¼ cup sugar until thick, then add gelatin, rum and vanilla. Pour into bowl with whites. Again with same beaters, whip ½ cup whipping cream until stiff. Fold cream, ¾ cup Macadamia Crunch Candy, egg yolks and whites smoothly together. Pour into pie shell. Chill until firm or about 3 hours. Whip remaining cream and spread gently over pie. Sprinkle evenly with remaining candy. Cover loosely. Chill.

MOCHA BUTTER CRUNCH PIE

Crust:
1 cup all-purpose flour
¼ teaspoon salt
⅓ cup dark brown sugar, packed
⅓ cup butter, cold
3 tablespoons bitter chocolate, finely chopped
¾ cup walnuts, finely chopped
2½ tablespoons water
1 teaspoon vanilla

Filling:
½-pound unsalted butter, cold
1 cup brown sugar
4 teaspoons instant coffee powder
2 teaspoons vanilla
3-ounces bitter chocolate, melted
4 eggs

Topping:
2 cups whipping cream, very cold
2 tablespoons plus 1 teaspoon instant coffee powder
½ cup powdered sugar
Grated chocolate for garnish

Serves 8 to 10.

To make the crust, combine flour, salt and brown sugar. With a pastry blender or two knives, cut in butter. Using a fork, stir in chopped chocolate and nuts. Mix the water with the vanilla. Toss with the crumb mixture. With floured fingers, press the crumbs into a 9-inch pie pan, including the rim. Bake for 15 to 20 minutes at 350°. Cool.

To make the filling, cream butter until fluffy. Beat in brown sugar, instant coffee and vanilla. When completely smooth, add the melted bitter chocolate. Stir until well-blended. Add eggs one at a time, beating for 3 to 4 minutes after each addition. Pour mixture into pie shell and chill for several hours.

To make topping, just before serving, combine the topping ingredients and whip until stiff enough to hold a shape. Place in a pastry bag using large star tip and pile large rosettes over top of pie. If you do not have a pastry bag, swirl whipped cream on top. Sprinkle with grated chocolate and serve.

EGGNOG POUND CAKE

2 tablespoons butter or margarine, softened
½ cup sliced almonds
1 package yellow cake mix
⅛ teaspoon nutmeg
1½ cups commercial eggnog
¼ cup butter or margarine, melted
2 eggs
2 tablespoons rum or
¼ teaspoon rum flavoring

Serves 8 to 10.

Generously grease a 10-inch tube or bundt pan with the softened butter. Press almonds against the buttered sides and bottom of pan.

Using an electric mixer or a wooden spoon, combine cake mix, nutmeg, eggnog, melted butter, eggs and rum in a large mixing bowl until blended. Beat batter until smooth and creamy (about 4 minutes at medium speed with electric mixer or about 450 strokes by hand). Pour batter into prepared pan. Bake at 350° for 45 to 55 minutes or until wooden skewer inserted in the thickest portion comes out clean. Cool in pan 10 minutes. Invert cake onto a rack and cool completely.

FESTIVE CAKE

Cake:
3 cups flour
1¾ cups sugar
1 teaspoon baking soda
1 teaspoon salt
1 teaspoon cinnamon
½ teaspoon nutmeg
⅛ teaspoon ground cloves
1 cup chopped almonds
3 eggs
¼ cup shortening
¾ cup vegetable oil
1 teaspoon almond extract
2 cups bananas, chopped or
2 medium bananas, chopped plus
4 tablespoons applesauce
1 8-ounce can crushed pineapple with juice

Cream Cheese Frosting:
1 3-ounce package cream cheese, softened
6 tablespoons butter, softened
2 cups powdered sugar, sifted
¼ teaspoon almond extract
½ teaspoon vanilla
1 tablespoon instant chocolate mix, optional

Serves 10 to 15.

Sift together flour, sugar, baking soda, salt, and spices into large bowl. Add almonds. Beat eggs slightly in a separate large bowl. Continuing to beat eggs, add shortening and oil, almond extract, bananas and pineapple with juice. Fold liquid mixture gently into dry ingredients. Do not beat. Spoon into well-oiled tube or bundt pan. Bake at 350° for 20 minutes. Reduce heat to 325° and bake for 45 minutes more or until cake tests done. Remove cake from oven and let stand 10 minutes before turning cake onto rack. Cool thoroughly.

To make frosting, beat cream cheese and butter together. Continue to stir, adding sugar, almond extract and vanilla. Add the chocolate if desired. If frosting is too thick, thin with coffee or cream to desired consistency. Pour over cake and serve.

TRIPLE SEED CAKE

Cake:
3 cups sifted flour
2½ teaspoons baking powder
¾ teaspoons nutmeg
1 teaspoon salt
⅔ cup shortening
2 cups sugar
4 eggs
1 cup milk
2 tablespoons orange rind, grated
1 tablespoon lemon rind, grated
1 tablespoon caraway seed
1 tablespoon poppy seed
1 tablespoon anise seed

Glaze:
1¼ cups powdered sugar, sifted
2 tablespoons orange juice
1 teaspoon lemon juice

Makes 10-inch cake.

Sift together flour, baking powder, nutmeg and salt. Set aside. Blend together shortening and sugar. Cream well. Add unbeaten eggs one at a time. Beat for one minute after each addition. Measure milk and add alternately with dry ingredients to the creamed mixture, beginning and ending with dry. Blend thoroughly after each addition on low speed with an electric mixer. Blend in orange and lemon rind. Grease well and lightly flour bottom only of 10-inch tube pan. Spread ¼ of batter into bottom of pan. Sprinkle with caraway seeds. Alternate remaining batter with poppy seeds and then anise seeds, ending with batter on top. Bake at 350° for 75 to 80 minutes. Let cool for 15 minutes in pan before removing. Combine glaze ingredients. Blend well. Pour over slightly warm cake.

HEAVENLY CARROT CAKE

Cake:
1⅓ cup sugar
4 eggs
1¼ cups oil
1¾ cups flour
2 teaspoons baking soda
1 teaspoon baking powder
1 teaspoon salt
3 teaspoons cinnamon
½ teaspoon ginger
1 teaspoon vanilla
1¾ cups carrots, grated
4-ounces crushed pineapple
1 cup coconut
½ cup nuts, chopped

Frosting:
½ cup butter, softened
8-ounces cream cheese, softened
1 pound powdered sugar

Serves 12.

Beat sugar, eggs and oil together until well-blended. Beat in flour, baking soda, baking powder, salt, cinnamon, ginger and vanilla. Fold in carrots, pineapple, coconut and nuts. Grease and flour three 8-inch round pans. Divide batter. Bake at 350° for 30 to 35 minutes. Cool 10 minutes. Remove from pans and cool completely. Blend frosting ingredients together until smooth. Frost.

CARROT BUNDT CAKE

Cake:
1½ cups vegetable oil
2 cups sugar
3 eggs
2½ cups flour
2 teaspoons baking soda
1 teaspoon salt
2 teaspoons cinnamon
1 cup coconut
1 cup pineapple, crushed and drained
1 cup carrots, grated
1 cup nuts, chopped

Topping:
1 cup sugar
¼ cup butter
1 teaspoon soda
1 tablespoon corn syrup
½ cup buttermilk

Serves 12.

In a large mixing bowl, beat together oil, sugar and eggs. Sift together flour, soda, salt and cinnamon. Add by thirds to egg mixture. Add coconut, pineapple, carrots and nuts.

Pour into a greased and floured bundt pan. Bake at 350° for 1½ hours. Let cool 10 minutes and remove from pan onto cake plate. Using a wooden skewer, poke holes in the top of cake.

Combine sugar, butter, soda, corn syrup and buttermilk in a saucepan. Bring to a boil, then simmer for 5 minutes. Remove from heat and slowly ladle over hot cake, allowing the topping to be absorbed into cake. Cool and serve.

FUDGEY CHOCOLATE TORTE AND CHOCOLATE GLAZE

Cake:
¾ cup butter
6 tablespoons cocoa
1 cup sugar, divided
⅔ cup blanched almonds, ground
2 tablespoons flour
3 eggs, separated
2 tablespoons water

Glaze:
2 tablespoons butter
2 tablespoons cocoa
2 tablespoons water
½ teaspoon vanilla
1 cup powdered sugar

Serves 8 to 10.

Grease and flour 9-inch layer cake pan. Melt butter in medium saucepan over low heat. Stir in cocoa and ¾ cup sugar. Blend until smooth. Remove from heat. Cool 5 minutes. Blend in almonds and flour. Beat in egg yolks one at a time. Stir in water. In medium bowl, beat egg whites until foamy. Gradually add remaining sugar, beating until soft peaks form. Gently fold chocolate mixture into egg whites, blending thoroughly. Pour into prepared pan and bake at 350° for 30 minutes or until tester comes out clean. Cool 10 minutes. Remove from pan onto wire rack. Cool completely. Invert cake onto serving plate.

To prepare glaze, melt butter in small saucepan over low heat. Add cocoa and water, stirring constantly until thickened. Do not boil. Remove from heat. Add vanilla. Gradually add powdered sugar and beat with whisk until smooth. Spread over top and sides of cake. Serve.

WILLIAMSBURG INN BLACK FOREST CHERRY TORTE

Chocolate Sponge Cake:
4 1-ounce squares unsweetened baking chocolate
1 cup milk
1 cup flour
½ teaspoon salt
4 egg yolks with whites reserved
2 cups powdered sugar
1 teaspoon vanilla

Cherry Filling:
1 16-ounce can water-packed tart red cherries, drained with liquid reserved
½ cup sugar
2½ tablespoons cornstarch
3 drops red food coloring
½ teaspoon almond flavoring
1 tablespoon butter

Cream Filling:
1 quart whipping cream
¼ cup powdered sugar
½ cup Kirshwasser (cherry brandy)

Chocolate Buttercream Frosting:
6 tablespoons butter
1 1-pound package powdered sugar, sifted (about 4¾ cups)
¼ cup light cream
1½ teaspoons vanilla
2 1-ounce squares unsweetened chocolate

Garnish:
Chocolate shavings
12-16 maraschino cherries

Serves 12.

To prepare sponge cake, melt chocolate with milk. Cool. Sift together flour and salt. Set aside. Cream together egg yolks, powdered sugar and vanilla. Add chocolate and milk mixture and flour mixture. Beat 4 egg whites until stiff. Fold into other ingredients. Generously grease and flour three 9-inch cake pans. Pour batter evenly between three cake pans. Bake at 325° for 25 minutes. Cool 10 minutes and remove to racks to cool further.

To make cherry filling, combine sugar, cornstarch and food coloring with cherry liquid and cook until thickened. Add almond flavoring and butter. Add cherries. Cool before using.

To prepare whipping cream filling, whip the cream adding ¼ cup powdered sugar gradually. Add ½ cup Kirshwasser. Refrigerate until needed.

To prepare frosting, cream butter, gradually add half the sugar, blending well. Beat in 2 tablespoons cream and vanilla. Gradually blend in remaining sugar, adding enough cream to thin to desired spreading consistency. Add melted and cooled chocolate, blending a little at a time.

To assemble cherry torte, with a plain ½-inch decorating tube, pipe three rings of chocolate buttercream frosting on the bottom layer, leaving enough space between each ring to fill with cherry filling. Place second cake layer over and sprinkle with Kirshwasser. Spread this layer with flavored whipped cream 1-inch thick. Put third layer on top and spread sides and top of torte with remaining cream. Sprinkle completely with chocolate shavings. Dust with powdered sugar. Decorate rim top with 12 to 16 rosettes (from buttercream frosting) and red maraschino cherries on top of each rosette. Keep refrigerated.

CHOCOLATE MOUSSE TORTE

The ultimate mousse.

7-ounces almond paste
1 tablespoon cocoa
5 eggs
6-ounces semi-sweet chocolate
2 teaspoons instant coffee
1 tablespoon brandy
2 tablespoons sugar
½ cup whipping cream

Serves 6.

Crumble almond paste into blender or food processor. Add cocoa and 2 eggs. Blend until smooth. Pour into greased, floured 9-inch springform pan. Bake at 350° for 15 minutes. Let cool. Melt chocolate in double boiler. Separate 2 eggs, setting aside whites. Break remaining egg into large bowl, add yolks, beat well. Blend in brandy, coffee and melted chocolate. In another bowl, whip egg whites, add sugar gradually, whipping until moist and stiff peaks form. Fold into chocolate mixture. Whip cream and fold into mixture, spread evenly over cooled cake and freeze. To serve, unmold and cut in very thin wedges.

BLINTZ TORTE

Well-baked tortes or meringues will keep several weeks if cooled well, then stored in tightly covered containers.

½ cup butter, softened
½ cup sugar
4 egg yolks, beaten
1 cup cake flour, sifted
Pinch of salt
1 teaspoon baking powder
5 tablespoons milk
1 teaspoon vanilla extract
4 egg whites
1 cup sugar
Cinnamon sugar
⅓ cup sliced almonds

Custard:
6 tablespoons sugar
1 tablespoon cornstarch
½ cup sour cream
3 egg yolks, lightly beaten
1 tablespoon butter
1 teaspoon vanilla extract
½ teaspoon almond extract

Garnish:
½ pint whipping cream, sweetened and whipped
Sliced strawberries

Serves 8 to 10.

Cream together butter and ½ cup sugar. Beat in egg yolks. Sift together flour, salt and baking powder. Add flour mixture to butter mixture alternately with milk. Add vanilla, mix thoroughly and pour into 2 well-greased and floured 8 or 9-inch layer pans. Set aside. In another bowl, beat egg whites until stiff and continue beating while gradually adding 1 cup sugar. Spread this meringue over batter in pans. Sprinkle meringue lightly with cinnamon sugar and almonds. Bake at 350° for 25 to 35 minutes or until golden brown. Cool 10 minutes and turn out onto cooling racks.

To prepare custard, combine sugar and cornstarch. Add sour cream. Stir into lightly beaten egg yolks and add butter. Cook this mixture in double boiler, stirring constantly until thickened. Remove from heat and cool. Add flavorings. Chill. Use as filling between the two torte layers. Assemble shortly before serving. Place one layer on a cake plate, meringue side down, and spread with custard. Place second layer on top of custard with meringue side up.

If desired, top with whipped cream and sliced strawberries. Store in refrigerator.

RUM ESPRESSO MOUSSE CAKE

5 tablespoons rum
1¼ cups strong espresso
3 tablespoons sugar
1 16-ounce day-old pound cake
2 teaspoons rum, optional
4 eggs, separated
1 teaspoon sugar
10-ounces semi-sweet chocolate chips
1 teaspoon butter
1 cup heavy cream
Chocolate covered coffee beans or walnuts for garnish

Serves 12.

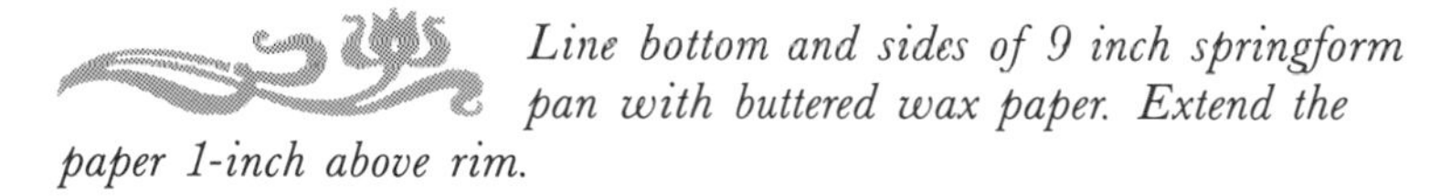

Line bottom and sides of 9 inch springform pan with buttered wax paper. Extend the paper 1-inch above rim.

Combine rum, espresso and 3 tablespoons sugar. Cut pound cake into ¼-inch slices. Dip in rum-espresso mixture. Place slices on bottom and along sides of baking pan. Reserve some slices for the top.

Beat egg yolks with 1 teaspoon sugar until yolks are pale yellow. Melt 6-ounces of chocolate; mix into beaten egg yolks. Cool. Whip egg whites until they form stiff peaks. Combine 1 tablespoon egg whites with yolks and chocolate. Fold in remaining whites and spoon mixture over pound cake. Cover with remaining slices of pound cake dipped in rum-coffee mixture and refrigerate overnight.

Next day, turn pan over onto a flat serving platter. Remove springform. Peel off wax paper.

For frosting, melt remaining 4-ounces chocolate with 1 teaspoon butter. Thinly cover entire surface of cake. Refrigerate until chocolate hardens, about 45 minutes. Whip cream with rum. Decorate cake using pastry bag and decorating tips. Garnish with chocolate coffee beans or walnuts. Cut with serrated knife.

MARKETPLACE MARJOLAINE

Time consuming but well worth the effort. Our chef recommends that marjolaine be refrigerated three full days before serving for best flavor and texture.

Meringue Layer:
1⅔ cups toasted almonds, sliced
½ cup plus 2 tablespoons sugar
¼ cup all-purpose flour
5 egg whites, room temperature
Pinch of salt
Pinch of cream of tartar

Almond Praline:
1 cup sugar
½ cup water
1 cup toasted almonds, sliced

Cream Filling:
1 cup whipping cream
2 tablespoons sugar
1 teaspoon vanilla

Chocolate Frosting:
9-ounces semi-sweet chocolate chips
1 cup sour cream
Sifted powdered sugar

Serves 10.

To make meringue, line bottom of jelly roll pan with parchment paper. Combine almonds, sugar and flour in processor or blender and process until almonds are finely ground. Beat egg whites with salt and cream of tartar in large bowl until stiff. Gently fold in almond mixture, being careful not to deflate egg whites. Spread meringue in prepared pan. Bake at 275° about 60 to 75 minutes or until just pliable. Cool in pan 5 minutes, then transfer to rack to cool completely. Discard parchment. Wrap meringue in plastic and refrigerate overnight.

To make praline, combine sugar and water in heavy medium saucepan over low heat. Cook until sugar is dissolved, shaking pan occasionally. Increase heat and cook until sugar is caramelized and turns deep mahogany. Immediately pour mixture onto ungreased baking sheet. Cool until firm. Break into pieces and place in processor or blender. Add almonds and grind to powder. Store in container with tight-fitting lid.

For cream filling, combine cream, sugar and vanilla in large bowl and whip until very stiff. Pour into strainer lined with linen towel or several layers of cheesecloth. Chill cream mixture overnight to drain. Blend half of cream with ½ cup almond praline powder. Reserve remaining praline powder for another use.

For frosting, combine chocolate and sour cream in top of double boiler set over barely simmering water. Stir with rubber spatula just until chocolate is melted and smooth. Do not overheat or mixture will

(Continued, Top Of Page 217

MARKETPLACE MARJOLANE

(Continued, From Page 216)

curdle. Cool slightly. Rewarm over hot water if frosting becomes too thick to spread.

To assemble, cut meringue layer crosswise into 4 equal rectangles. Place 1 rectangle on platter. Spread with praline cream. Top with second meringue layer. Spread top and sides with some of chocolate frosting. Refrigerate until chocolate sets or about 20 minutes. Spread second layer of frosting on top. Add third meringue and spread top and sides with chocolate. Refrigerate until chocolate sets. Spread with remaining cream filling. Top with fourth meringue layer. Coat top and sides of marjolaine with remaining chocolate frosting. Refrigerate until chocolate sets. Cover with plastic wrap and refrigerate at least 24 hours. Just before serving, dust top with sifted powdered sugar.

PAVLOVA

Red, ripe strawberries emerge in a pyramid fashion to top off this delicate Pavlova.

6 egg whites, room temperature
Pinch of salt
2 cups sugar
1½ teaspoons vinegar
1½ teaspoons vanilla
1 pint whipping cream, whipped and sweetened
1 quart or more fresh strawberries, sliced

Serves 6 to 8.

Beat egg whites with salt at high speed until soft peaks form. Add sugar, 1 tablespoon at a time, beating well after each addition. Fold in vinegar and vanilla.

Smooth mixture into 8-inch circle on ungreased cookie sheet. Smooth top. Bake for 45 minutes at 300°. Turn oven off and let set for 1 hour with oven door shut. Remove from oven and cool. Fill pavlova with cream and top with fruit.

AMARETTO CHIFFON CHEESECAKE

Crust:
1¾ cups fine graham cracker crumbs
¼ cup minced walnuts
½ teaspoon ground cinnamon
½ cup butter, melted

Filling:
3 eggs, beaten
2 8-ounce packages cream cheese, softened
1 cup sugar
¼ teaspoon salt
1 teaspoon vanilla
1 tablespoon Amaretto
½ teaspoon almond extract
3 cups sour cream

Nougatine:
½ cup almonds, sliced
½ cup sugar
2 tablespoons water

Serves 12.

To make crust, thoroughly mix together all crust ingredients in bowl. Press onto bottom and sides of a 9-inch springform pan. The crust should be about 1¾-inches high on the sides.

To prepare filling, combine eggs, cream cheese, sugar, salt, vanilla, Amaretto and almond extract in a large bowl and blend well. Beat until smooth, with an electric mixer, about 2 minutes. Blend in the sour cream. Pour the filling into the crust and bake at 375° for 35 minutes or until set. Cool. Chill thoroughly, about 4 to 5 hours or overnight.

For nougatine, toast almonds for 6 to 8 minutes at 350°. Combine sugar and water in saucepan. Cook until sugar caramelizes. Stir in nuts. Remove from heat and pour onto buttered baking sheet. When cooled, break into small pieces. When cheesecake has been chilled, sprinkle with nougatine.

STRAWBERRY-GLAZED CREAM CHEESECAKE

Crust:
¾ cup coarsely ground walnuts
¾ cup finely crushed graham crackers
3 tablespoons melted unsalted butter

Filling:
4 8-ounce packages cream cheese, at room temperature
4 eggs
1¼ cup sugar
1 tablespoon fresh lemon juice
2 teaspoons vanilla

Topping:
2 cups sour cream
¼ cup sugar
1 teaspoon vanilla

Strawberry Glaze:
1 quart medium strawberries
1 12-ounce jar red raspberry jelly
1 tablespoon cornstarch
¼ cup Cointreau
¼ cup water

Serves 10 to 12.

Position rack in center of oven. Lightly butter 9 or 10-inch springform pan.

To make crust, combine walnuts, graham crackers and butter. Press compactly onto bottom of pan.

To prepare filling, beat cream cheese in large bowl of electric mixer until smooth. Add eggs, sugar, lemon juice and vanilla and beat thoroughly. Spoon over crust. Set pan on baking sheet to catch butter that may drip out. Bake 10-inch cake 40 to 45 minutes or 9-inch cake 50 to 55 minutes at 350°. Cake may rise slightly and crack in several areas. It will settle again, cracks will minimize and topping will cover it up. Remove from oven and let stand at room temperature 15 minutes. Retain oven temperature at 350°.

To make topping, combine sour cream, sugar and vanilla and blend well. Cover and refrigerate. When cake has finished baking, spoon topping over, starting at the center and extending to within ½-inch of edge. Return to oven and bake 5 minutes longer. Let cool, then refrigerate cheesecake at least 24 hours or preferably 2 to 3 days.

To prepare glaze, several hours before serving, wash and hull berries and let dry completely on paper towels. Combine a little jelly with cornstarch in saucepan and mix well. Add remaining jelly, Cointreau and water and cook over medium heat until thickened and clear, about 5 minutes. Cool to lukewarm, stirring occasionally.

Using knife, loosen cake from pan. Remove springform. Arrange berries pointed end up over top of cake. Spoon glaze over berries, allowing some to drip down sides of cake. Return to refrigerator until the glaze is set.

WHITE CHOCOLATE RASPBERRY CHEESECAKE

This delicious combination is an elegant ending for any meal.

Crust:
1¼ cups shortbread cookie crumbs, finely ground
¼ cup ground almonds, about 1-ounce
2 tablespoons sugar
⅛ teaspoon almond extract
3 tablespoons or more unsalted butter, melted

Filling:
6-ounces white chocolate, finely chopped
3 8-ounce packages cream cheese, room temperature
½ pound Neufchatel cheese, room temperature
5 large eggs, room temperature
¾ cup sugar
3 tablespoons flour
1 teaspoon vanilla
¼ teaspoon almond extract

Glaze:
7 tablespoons whipping cream
8-ounces white chocolate, finely chopped
¼ cup raspberry jam, melted and strained
Toasted sliced almonds
Fresh raspberries
1 12-ounce bag frozen unsweetened raspberries, thawed, pureed and strained

Serves 12.

For crust, preheat oven to 350°. Mix first four ingredients in small bowl. Blend in enough butter to bind crumbs. Press mixture firmly onto bottom of 10-inch springform pan. Bake 10 minutes. Transfer to rack and cool completely. Reduce oven temperature to 325°.

For filling, melt chocolate in double boiler over simmering water, stirring until smooth. Cool to lukewarm. Using electric mixer, beat cheeses in large bowl until smooth. Blend in eggs, one at a time. Mix in sugar, flour, vanilla and almond extract. Stir 1 cup of mixture into lukewarm white chocolate; mix into remaining filling in bowl.

Pour filling over crust. Bake until cheesecake is firm around edges but still moves slightly in center when pan is shaken, about 40 minutes. Transfer to rack and cool completely. Cover and refrigerate overnight.

For glaze, bring cream to simmer in heavy small saucepan over low heat. Add chocolate and stir until smooth.

Spoon glaze over top of cheesecake. Using spatula, spread glaze slightly over edge. Refrigerate until glaze is set.

Brush jam around sides of cheesecake. Press almonds onto sides, covering completely. (Can be prepared 2 days ahead. Cover and refrigerate.) Arrange raspberries in center of cheesecake if desired. Serve with raspberry pureé.

LEMON CHIFFON CHEESECAKE

Crust:
4 cups graham cracker crumbs
1 cup butter, melted

Filling:
¼ cup cold water
2 tablespoons unflavored gelatin
¾ cup sugar
5 egg yolks
pinch of salt
⅓ cup milk, scalded
1½ pounds cream cheese, room temperature
⅓ cup fresh lemon juice
¼ cup Grand Marnier
2 drops vanilla
5 egg whites, room temperature
½ cup sugar
finely grated peel of 2 lemons

Serves 12.

To make crust, blend crumbs and melted butter in large bowl. Set aside ⅓ cup of mixture. Press remainder into bottom and sides of 10-inch springform pan. Bake at 350° until firm, about 12 to 15 minutes. Let cool completely on rack.

For filling, pour cold water into cup. Sprinkle with gelatin. Let stand until softened, about 5 minutes. Combine ¾ cup sugar with yolks and salt in top of double boiler and beat well. Set over gently simmering water. Gradually add hot milk, beating constantly until thick, about 5 minutes. Add softened gelatin and stir until completely dissolved. Let cool to lukewarm.

Beat cream cheese in large bowl until smooth. Beat in small amount of yolk mixture, then fold in remaining yolks. Fold in lemon juice, Grand Marnier and vanilla. Beat egg whites in large bowl until soft peaks form. Gradually add ½ cup sugar beating until stiff but not dry. Fold into cheese mixture. Turn filling into crust smoothing top. Sprinkle with reserved crumb mixture and lemon peel. Chill until firm, at least 6 hours or overnight.

MARVELOUS MOCHA CHEESECAKE

Cocoa-crumb Crust:
1⅓ cups graham cracker crumbs
3 tablespoons sugar
3 tablespoons unsweetened cocoa powder
⅓ cup butter or margarine, melted

Cheesecake:
4 3-ounce packages cream cheese, at room temperature
¾ cup sugar
2 eggs
1 tablespoon coffee-flavored liqueur
1 teaspoon vanilla extract
1 cup sour cream
1 1-ounce square unsweetened baking chocolate, grated

Mocha Crown:
1½ teaspoons instant coffee powder
2 tablespoons boiling water
4 1-ounce squares semi-sweet baking chocolate
4 eggs, separated
⅓ cup sugar
1 tablespoon coffee-flavored liqueur or rum
½ teaspoon vanilla extract

Garnish:
1 cup heavy cream or whipping cream, whipped
¾ cup blanched almonds, toasted & sliced

Serves 12.

To prepare crust, combine crumbs, sugar, cocoa powder and butter or margarine. Press mixture firmly on bottom and up side of a 9-inch springform pan. Bake 10 minutes at 350°. Place on rack to cool.

To make cheesecake, in large bowl, beat cream cheese with electric mixer on high speed until light and fluffy. Gradually beat in sugar. Add eggs, one at a time, beating well after each addition. Add liqueur and vanilla. Turn into prepared crust. Bake 30 minutes at 350°. Cool on rack 10 minutes. Gently spread sour cream over cheesecake. Sprinkle with grated chocolate. Refrigerate 30 minutes.

To prepare mocha crown, in top of double boiler over hot but not boiling water, dissolve coffee powder in 2 tablespoons boiling water. Add chocolate, stirring until chocolate is melted and mixture is blended. Remove from heat. In a medium bowl, beat egg whites with electric mixer until stiff. Set aside. Beat egg yolks in a large bowl until thick and pale. Gradually beat in sugar. Add chocolate mixture about ¼ cup at a time, beating well after each addition. Beat in coffee-flavored liqueur or rum and vanilla. Gently fold in beaten egg whites by hand.

Gently spread mocha crown over refrigerated cheesecake. Refrigerate until firm, about 2 to 3 hours. Loosen and remove side of pan. Place cheesecake on a serving plate. Spoon whipped cream over top of cake. Sprinkle almonds around edge.

NECTARINE ICE CREAM CHEESECAKE

A delightful fresh fruit dessert.

Cheesecake:
1½-pounds fresh nectarines
1 8-ounce package cream cheese, softened
½ cup sugar
¼ teaspoon salt
1 tablespoon lemon juice
½ teaspoon grated lemon rind
Crumb coating
1 cup whipped cream

Crumb Coating:
½ cup fine graham cracker crumbs
1 tablespoon sugar
1 tablespoon butter

Serves 6.

Dice nectarines to measure approximately 2½ cups. Blend until smooth. Blend sugar, salt, softened cream cheese, lemon juice, and rind. Mix until smooth. Gradually blend in nectarine puree. Mix until well-blended. Turn into loaf pan. Freeze until solid, about 2 hours.

To prepare crumb coating, combine graham cracker crumbs with 1 tablespoon sugar. Melt butter, add crumb mixture and stir over low heat until lightly browned, about 5 minutes. Beat cream to soft peaks and set aside. Break frozen mixture into chunks and place in chilled bowl. Beat at low speed until smooth, then at high speed until light and fluffy. Fold in whipped cream. Turn half of crumb mixture into 8-inch spring form pan. Spoon ice cream mixture over crumbs in an even layer. Sprinkle with remaining crumbs. Freeze until firm. Store in refrigerator 15 to 20 minutes before serving. Swirl extra whipped cream in rosettes on top and decorate with sliced nectarines.

KAHLUA FUDGE CHEESECAKE

Crust:
1½ cups chocolate cookie wafers, crushed
⅓ cup butter, melted

Filling:
1 8-ounce package cream cheese, softened
¼ cup sugar
½ cup cocoa
2 large eggs
5 tablespoons Kahlua or coffee liqueur
¼ cup extra-strong coffee
1 teaspoon vanilla

Topping:
1 cup whipping cream, chilled
2 tablespoons sugar
1 tablespoon Kahlua or coffee liqueur
Unsweetened chocolate, shaved

Serves 10 to 12.

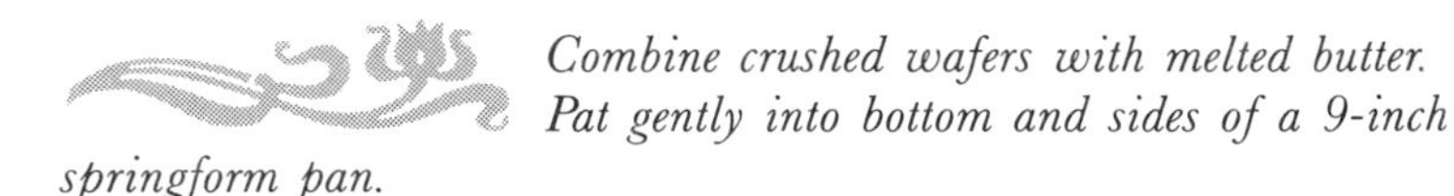

Combine crushed wafers with melted butter. Pat gently into bottom and sides of a 9-inch springform pan.

To make filling, combine cream cheese and sugar in large bowl. Beat with an electric mixer until light and well-blended. Add cocoa and eggs, beating until well-blended. Stir in Kahlua, coffee and vanilla. Pour into prepared pan and bake at 375° for 25 minutes. Remove from oven and cool. Chill 6 to 8 hours. Remove from pan.

To make topping, whip cream with sugar and Kahlua. Top cake with flavored cream. Garnish with shaved chocolate.

GRAND MARNIER MOUSSE

1 tablespoon unflavored gelatin
½ cup Grand Marnier
3 eggs, separated
½ cup sugar
1 cup whipping cream
12 lady fingers

Serves 6.

Soften gelatin in Grand Marnier. Drop egg yolks and sugar in small bowl placed over hot water. Beat 5 minutes until thick and pale. Stir in gelatin. Beat egg whites until stiff. Fold into gelatin. Beat cream until stiff. Fold into gelatin and egg white mixture. Line bowl or individual serving dishes with lady fingers. Spoon in mousse. Cover with plastic wrap. Chill 6 hours or overnight.

POACHED PEARS WITH AMARETTO CUSTARD

Poached Pears:
2 cups sugar
6 cups water
Peel of 1 lemon, cut in 1 long peel
1 tablespoon lemon juice
2 cloves
½ cinnamon stick
2 Bosc or Anjou pears, slightly underripe and preferably with long stems

Amaretto Custard:
2 large egg yolks
3 tablespoons sugar
½ teaspoon cornstarch
¾ cup heavy cream
2 tablespoons Amaretto
½ to 1 teaspoon lemon juice
Powdered amaretti for garnish

Serves 2.

To poach pears, combine sugar with water, lemon peel, lemon juice, cloves and cinnamon stick in a deep 3-quart pot. Bring to a boil. While the poaching syrup is cooking, peel pears, trimming the bottom so that they stand upright. Immediately place them into a bowl of cold water to which a little lemon juice has been added.

When the syrup is boiling, add the pears and cover the pot. Keep the liquid at a rolling boil so that the pears are constantly moving and cooking evenly throughout. Cook for 20 to 30 minutes or until pears are translucent and offer no resistance when pierced with toothpick. Remove from water and allow to cool.

If pears are prepared the day before, cover them with plastic wrap and refrigerate, but bring them to room temperature before serving. The poaching liquid can be frozen and reused.

To prepare custard, place the egg yolks in a mixing bowl and beat, gradually adding sugar until mixture is a pale yellow and has doubled in volume; about 3 minutes. Beat in cornstarch. Warm the cream and slowly beat into the yolk mixture. Pour into a heavy enameled saucepan and set over moderate heat. Stir the custard continually with a wire whisk. If custard begins to steam at any point, remove from heat and whisk until it has cooled slightly. (It must not even reach a simmer.) When the custard has thickened enough to heavily coat a wooden spoon, about 8 minutes, remove it from the heat. Add the Amaretto and lemon juice to taste. Transfer to a small mixing bowl and whisk for a few minutes to cool. When completely cooled, place a piece of plastic wrap directly on the surface of the custard and refrigerate. The sauce can be prepared the day before.

Place a poached pear on a small serving plate. Spoon Amaretto Custard around the base and over the top. Dust lightly with powdered amaretti (Italian macaroons) ground to a powder in the food processor or blender. Serve.

APPLE-CALVADOS CHERRY CRISP

A unique flavor combination of cherries and apples.

6-ounces dried tart cherries
⅓ cup calvados, (apple brandy)
6 cups apples, peeled and sliced
1 cup all-purpose flour
¾ cup sugar
½ teaspoon ground cinnamon
¼ teaspoon salt
½ cup unsalted butter, softened and cut into bits, (1 stick)
Whipped cream flavored with vanilla or vanilla ice cream

Serves 6 to 8.

Combine dried cherries with calvados and set aside for at least 10 minutes. Mix marinated cherries and remaining calvados with the apples and place evenly in a deep 7-inch by 9-inch greased baking dish. Combine remaining ingredients and mix with your hands until the mixture is the texture of rough meal. Spread evenly over the apples and cherries, smoothing with your hands. Bake for 35 minutes at 350° or until the top begins to turn color and the mixture is bubbling. Serve with flavored whipped cream or ice cream.

FRESH FRUIT WITH AMARETTO CREAM

Especially good with strawberries, blueberries or green grapes.

1½ tablespoons Amaretto
2 tablespoons dark brown sugar, packed
½ cup sour cream
2 cups fresh fruit

Serves 4.

In a small mixing bowl, combine Amaretto and brown sugar. Add sour cream and mix well. Prepare at least 2 hours before serving. Stir occasionally to dissolve brown sugar.

Slice fruit into bite-size pieces and arrange in sherbet glasses or small dishes. Drizzle with sauce.

COLD LEMON SOUFFLÉ

Soufflé:
2 envelopes unflavored gelatin
¾ cup cold water
4 to 5 lemons
8 eggs, separated
½ teaspoon salt
2 cups sugar
¼ teaspoon nutmeg
¼ teaspoon cinnamon
¼ teaspoon mace
1 teaspoon almond extract
2 tablespoons Grand Marnier or ¾ teaspoon orange extract
2 cup whipping cream
½ cup powdered sugar

Spiced Whipped Cream:
1 cup whipping cream
6 tablespoons powdered sugar
1 teaspoon vanilla
⅛ teaspoon cinnamon
⅛ teaspoon nutmeg
⅛ teaspoon mace

Candied Lemon Shreds:
¼ cup lemon shreds
¼ cup sugar
¼ cup water
1 tablespoon Grand Marnier
1 whole allspice
1 1-inch vanilla bean piece

Serves 10.

To prepare soufflé, fold a 30-inch strip of foil in half, lengthwise. Tie it around the outside of a 6-cup soufflé dish to make a collar which stands above the rim of the dish.

Soften the gelatin in cold water.

Cut ¼ cup long shreds of lemon peel from fresh lemon and set aside. Squeeze the lemons to obtain 1 cup juice.

Combine the egg yolks, lemon juice, salt, 1 cup sugar, nutmeg, cinnamon and mace in a heavy saucepan. Cook on low heat, stirring constantly, until slightly thickened. Stir in the gelatin until dissolved and ½ teaspoon almond extract. Pour into the gelatin mixture. Pour into a large bowl. Cool. Stir in the Grand Marnier.

Beat the egg whites until foamy. Gradually add 1 cup sugar and beat until stiff peaks form. Whip the cream with the powdered sugar and ½ teaspoon almond extract. Fold the egg whites and cream into the gelatin mixture. Pour into the soufflé dish. Chill 6 hours or overnight.

To prepare spiced whipped cream, whip the cream with the sugar until stiff. Fold in the vanilla, cinnamon, nutmeg and mace.

To prepare candied lemon shreds, combine the lemon shreds, sugar, water, Grand Marnier, allspice and vanilla bean in a saucepan and simmer until peel is transparent. Remove the allspice and vanilla bean. Drain the lemon shreds on a cake rack.

To serve the soufflé, cut the string and carefully remove the foil collar. Decorate top of soufflé with spice whipped cream pressed through a pastry bag with a large star tip. Garnish the center with the candied lemon shreds.

COOKIES AND CREAM ICE CREAM

3 egg yolks
1 14-ounce can sweetened condensed milk, (not evaporated milk)
2 tablespoons water
4 teaspoons vanilla
1 cup chocolate sandwich cookies, coarsely crushed
2 cups whipping cream, whipped

Makes 2 quarts.

In large bowl, beat egg yolks. Stir in condensed milk, water and vanilla. Fold in cookies and whipped cream. Pour into 9 by 5-inch loaf pan or 2-quart container. Cover and freeze for 6 hours.

DEVONSHIRE CREAM

The Northwest produces some of the greatest of all raspberries. This most elegant of fruits — cherished for its delicate flavor — looks quite festive when layered with Devonshire cream.

1-pound cream cheese, softened
¾ cup sugar
⅓ cup milk
2 tablespoons fresh orange juice
2 teaspoons vanilla
1½ cups sour cream
Raspberries or other fresh fruit

Serves 6.

Beat together cream cheese, sugar, milk, orange juice and vanilla until smooth. Fold in sour cream. Carefully layer Devonshire cream and fresh fruit in parfait glasses. Chill and serve.

PEACH MACAROONS

6 to 8 peaches
12 macaroon cookies
½ cup raspberry jam
¼ cup Amaretto
Butter

Serves 6 to 8.

Halve peaches and pit. Scrape out part of peach to enlarge cavity. Chop scooped out peach. Crumble 4 macaroon cookies and add to chopped peach. Add jam and Amaretto. Stir gently to mix. Place peaches in 9 by 13-inch baking dish (cavity side up). Divide mixture equally in peach cavities. Dot with butter. Bake for 20 minutes at 350°. Serve warm with macaroon cookies.

ROCKY ROAD FUDGE BARS

Bar:
½ cup butter
1 square unsweetened chocolate
1 cup sugar
1 cup flour
½ to 1 cup walnuts, chopped
1 teaspoon baking powder
1 teaspoon vanilla
2 eggs

Filling:
6-ounces cream cheese
½ cup sugar
2 tablespoons flour
¼ cup butter

Filling (continued):
1 egg
½ teaspoon vanilla
¼ cup walnuts, chopped
1 6-ounce package chocolate chips

Frosting:
2 cups miniature marshmallows
¼ cup butter
1 square unsweetened chocolate
2-ounces cream cheese
¼ cup milk
1-pound powdered sugar
1 teaspoon vanilla

Makes 36 bars.

Grease and flour 9 by 13-inch pan. Over low heat, melt butter and chocolate in a large saucepan. Add remaining bar ingredients. Mix well and spread in pan. In small bowl mix cream cheese, sugar, flour, butter, egg, and vanilla until smooth and fluffy. Stir in nuts and spread over bar layer. Sprinkle top with chocolate chips. Bake for 25 to 30 minutes at 350°. Sprinkle with marshmallows and bake 2 minutes longer. In large saucepan, melt butter, chocolate, cream cheese, and milk over low heat. Stir in powdered sugar and vanilla until smooth. Immediately pour over bar. Cool. Serve at room temperature or chilled.

ALMOST REAL ROCA

40 soda crackers
1 cup brown sugar
1 cup butter
2 cups semi-sweet chocolate chips
½ to 1 cup almonds, ground

Makes 80 pieces.

Line 9 by 13-inch jelly roll pan with foil. Coat with vegetable spray or grease lightly. Line the pan with crackers, leaving space between each one.

Boil sugar and butter for 3 minutes. Pour over crackers. Bake at 350° for 5 minutes. Remove from oven and sprinkle with chocolate chips, spreading as they melt. Sprinkle with almonds. Cool. Break into bite-size pieces and store in a cool place.

CHOCOMINT CREAMS

½ cup butter or margarine
1-ounce unsweetened chocolate
1 cup flour
½ cup sugar
1 15-ounce can sweetened condensed milk
1½ cups flaked coconut
½ cup pecans, chopped
1 package solid chocolate mint wafers

Makes 6 dozen 1-inch squares.

Melt butter or margarine with unsweetened chocolate. Blend in flour and sugar. Mix well. Spread into a 9-inch square buttered pan. Bake for 10 minutes at 350°.

Mix together condensed milk, coconut, and nuts. Spread over baked base. Bake 25 to 30 minutes at 350° until filling is set.

Remove from oven and spread chocolate mints over filling. Let stand for 5 minutes and spread chocolate mints evenly. Cool.

Before the icing is completely hardened, score with a sharp knife to make slicing easier. Cut into 1-inch squares.

EXQUISITE MINT STICKS

Bar:
2 1-ounce squares unsweetened baking chocolate
½ cup butter or margarine
2 eggs
1 cup sugar
¼ teaspoon peppermint extract
½ cup sifted all-purpose flour
Dash of salt
½ cup unblanched almonds, chopped

Filling:
2 tablespoons butter or margarine, softened
1 cup powdered sugar
1 tablespoon cream
¾ teaspoon peppermint extract

Glaze:
1 1-ounce square unsweetened chocolate
1 tablespoon butter or margarine

Makes 48 sticks.

Melt chocolate and butter over hot water. Beat eggs until frothy. Stir in sugar, chocolate mixture and peppermint extract. Add flour, salt and almonds. Mix thoroughly. Bake in ungreased 9 by 9-inch pan for 20 to 25 minutes at 350°. Cool.

To prepare filling, work butter into powdered sugar, cream and peppermint extract. Stir until smooth. Spread on top of pastry in a thin coating.

Put filling-covered cake in the refrigerator to cool until the filling is firm.

To make glaze, melt chocolate and butter over hot water. Mix thoroughly and dribble over the cool, firm filling. Tilt cake back and forth until the glaze covers the surface. Refrigerate for at least 5 minutes. Cut into ¾-inch by 2¼-inch sticks.

MOCHA TRUFFLES

1 6-ounce package chocolate chips
⅔ cup butter, softened
1 egg yolk
1¼ cups powdered sugar
1 tablespoon rum
1 teaspoon instant coffee powder
Chocolate shot (sprinkles)
Confectioners' paper cups

Makes 2½ dozen.

Melt chocolate chips in the top of a double boiler over hot (not boiling) water. Remove from heat and set aside to cool briefly. Cream butter, egg yolk and powdered sugar. Add rum, instant coffee powder and melted chocolate chips. Chill 1 to 2 hours in refrigerator or until mixture can be formed into balls. Roll into 1-inch balls, then in chocolate shot or sprinkles. Place in paper cups on a plate. Refrigerate 1 to 2 hours before serving. They will keep a couple of weeks in the refrigerator covered with plastic wrap.

RUM TRUFFLES

7-ounces bittersweet Swiss chocolate, cut into 1-inch pieces
½ cup whipping cream
2 tablespoons butter
¾ cup powdered sugar, measured then sifted
2 egg yolks
1 to 2 tablespoons dark rum or to taste
Unsweetened cocoa and/or toasted nuts, coarsely chopped
Confectioners' paper cups

Makes 3 dozen.

Combine chocolate, whipping cream and butter in top of double boiler over simmering water. Add sugar and yolks and whisk until smooth. Remove from heat and add rum to taste. Place in flat glass dish and chill until pliable, about 2 hours in refrigerator or 1 hour in freezer. Shape into small 1-inch balls and roll in cocoa and/or nuts. Place in confectioners' paper cups and chill until hardened. They will keep for a couple of weeks in the refrigerator covered with plastic wrap.

BAKED FUDGE

Imagine. . . fudge without graininess or sugar-texture! The secret lies in this easy oven-baked method of preparation.

2 cups sugar
4 eggs, room temperature
½ cup flour
½ cup unsweetened cocoa
1 cup butter
1 cup pecans or walnuts, chopped
2 teaspoons vanilla
Unsweetened whipped cream for garnish

Serves 8 to 10.

Beat sugar and eggs together until mixture forms a slowly dissolving ribbon when beaters are lifted. Sift flour and cocoa into mixture and blend well. Stir in melted butter, nuts and vanilla. Do not overmix. Spread batter evenly into 8 by 10-inch baking pan. Set into larger pan, adding enough boiling water to larger pan to come halfway up sides. Bake at 350° for about 1 hour until fudge is firm and knife inserted in the center comes out moist but clean. Let cool. Cut into squares. Serve with whipped cream.

INDEX

B *(continued)*

C

C *(continued)*

D

I

K

L

M

M *(continued)*

INDEX *(continued)*

S (continued)

T

ACKNOWLEDGEMENTS

The Junior League of Yakima dedicates Northwest Fresh to those whose commitment to excellence have made this book possible. We thank the members, their family and friends who have contributed recipes and those who gave so generously of their time and talents in testing these recipes to assure the quality of this cookbook. A special note of gratitude to Bill Robertson, for her generous support of Northwest Fresh.

Jamie Abbenhaus
Nancy Abbenhaus
Patricia Ackley
Inez Adkison
Maureen Adkison
Carol Aiken
Michele Alexander
Judy Allen
Joanne Almon
Sherry Altena
Debbie Anderson
Janis Anderwald
Jill Antonius
Okie Applegate
Molly Archer
Rosanne Bacon
Suzanne Bacon
Augusta Baird
Deborah Baldwin
Patricia Ball
Sally Baney
Diana Barnhill
Carol Barrett
Martha Barringer
Cynthia Barwin
Rosemarie Beasley
Anne Berg
Helen Berghoff
Karen Bernd
Virginia Bice
Judi Black
Judy Blair
Ronna Blakeley
Connie Bloxom
Bernice Bohoskey
Ann Bongiani
Barbara Bordeaux
Mary Lou Boyd
Delores Brackett
Annie Bradford
Mary-Beth Bradley
Jackie Brassington
Meg Brooks
Betsy Broom
Linda Brown
Hilde Brule
Dode Brundage
Patricia Busse
Patti Butte
Doug Button
Barbara Butts
Cafe European
Karen Cameron
Jessica Camp
Lori Campbell
Teresa Camper
Diane Carey
Mary Carhart
Barbara Carlson
Christina Carlson
Karin Carlson
Evie Chambers
Monnie Jo Chaney
Nancy Charron
Alice Clark
Patty Clark
Barbara Clevenger
Susan Coddington
Nancy Colleran
Janine Connell
Jeanne Conners
Adele Connors
Suzanne Conrad
Kay Cook
Barbara Cooper
Myrna Corbett
Cheryl Cornell
Sue Crossland
Marie Courtney
Kathryn Culpepper
Cheryl Dale
Gail Davis
Lyndal Davis
Bettie de Beauchamp
Carol Ann de La Chapelle
Deli de Pasta
Lorna Dempsey
Linda DePew
Delores Desserault
Doris Dickensen
Barbara Ditter
Sonja Dodge
Debbie Dolquist
Rhonda Dolsen
Ruth Dolsen
Virginia Doudna
Sally Douglas
Betty Dreher
Doris Drumhiller
Linda Drumhiller
Bobbie Dwinell
Pam Eakes
Mary Eakin
Cindy Edgerton
Jeanna Edgerton
Kim Ehrman
Sara Eickerman
Hilary Eilmes
Gun Elofson
Becky Erickson
Caroline Erickson
Julie Erickson
Pat Erickson
Mary Evenson
Cheryl Falk
Connie Farina
Nancy Farrell
Barb Feasey
Vana Fessler
Racial Fields
Carol Fischer
Mary Fishback
Victoria Flower
Jayne Floyd
Barbara Forrest
Betty Fowler
Bunker Frank
Heather Frank
Jane Freitag
Gasperetti's
Patricia Gates
Lois Gervais
Ellen Gibson
Janet Gifford
Betty Gilbert

ACKNOWLEDGEMENTS *(continued)*

Virginia Gilbert
Judi Gilmore
Linda Gilmore
Lynn Gilmore
Gail Gilson
Mary Gladson
Janet Gonzalez
Carolyn Graden
Kiki Graf
Joanne Marquis-Gress
Michele Gress
Geraldine Guie
Mary Ann Hageman
Lenore Hains
Hale'Aina
Gayle Hall
Marie Halverson
Cherie Hanses
Frances Harris
Rosemary Harris
Anne Harrison
Kari Hatteberg
Susan Hattrup
Karen Hauser
Jan Haven
Marge Hawkes
Karen Hefner
Helen Helliesen
Jackie Helliesen
Rita Henderson
Robin Hendrickson
Peggy Henretig
Dottie Hildebrand
Karen Hill
Linda Hill
Ginger Hislop
Helen Mary Holt
Felicia Holtzinger
Sara Holtzinger
Shirley Hood
Teedie Hornby
Gladys Howard
Cindy Hubert
LeeAnn Hughes
Shirley Irwin
Maren Ivy
Christine Jackson
Kremiere Jackson
Terry Jackson
Donna Janovitch
Mauria Jensen
Jolene Jewett
Cindy Johnson
Linda Eakin Johnson
Mary Johnson
Sarah Judd
Renee Kabrich
Laurie Kanyer
Kay Keith
Karin Kerns
Karen Kershaw
Sally Kincaid
Debbie Kinder
Linda Kinney
Mary Kowalsky
Melissa Labberton
Denise LaBissioniere
Joy Larson
Kristy Larson
Nancy Leahy
Janet LeCocq
Tammy Lemaster
Karen Lenz
Jean Lewis
Peggy Lewis
Rhea Lewis
Joan Lindeman
Julie Linker
Lucy Linn
Linda Linneweh
Kathi Lofthouse
Kay Long
Kirby Long
Chris Losee
Lumi Loudon
Mardi Lundgren
Jan Luring
Darlene Lust
Sally Lust
Betty Rae Lynch
Lynette Lynch
Scotty Lyon
JoAnn McCarthy
Linda McIntyre
Barbara McKinney
Diana McLachlan
Roberta McMurray
Jane McNeal
Elizabeth Maher
Pam Manchester
Louise Marble
Marlyn Marble
Martha Marchand
Maria Marek
Sarah Marley
Debbie Marsing
Mary Virginia Maxwell
Alys Means
Nancy Melville
Ginny Mercy
Kathi Mercy
Eileen Merrell
Nancy Meyer
Ann Miller
Winifred Miller
Paula Monahan
Suzanne Monson
Debbie Moorer
Meg Morgan
Ruth Moser
Rebecca Mulalley-Thacker
Diane Murphy
JoRee Murphy
Mary Anne Murray
Marjorie Muzzall
Pat Myers
Judy Nagle
Kristine Nagle
Marcie Nashem
Lynn Nathe
Raney Naughton
Susan Naughton
Nancy Nesvig
Erma Nettleship
Mackay Neumann
JoAnne Newhouse
901 Pasta
Bea Noel
Teri Norman
Kathe Noyes
Margaret Nutley
Margaret O'Claire
Dorothy Olafson
Kathleen O'Meara Wyman
Victoria Onstad
Jan Overvold
Kerri Paxton
Jerry Pardo
Brad Patterson
Mary Jo Perez
Michelle Perkins
Donna Perry
Erwina Peterson
Dorothy Picatti
Janice Picatti
Mary Jo Pinnell
Lisa Plath
Lynn Plath
Mary Kay Pleger
Karen Pratt
Rosemary Preacher
Doretta Prentice

ACKNOWLEDGEMENTS *(continued)*

Lauren Price
Kate Putney
Lynn Quesenbury
Anne Rankin
Barbara Rankin
Jean Ratcliff
Harriet Redman
Jean Reed
Joan Gammie Reid
Sue Rich
Liann Richardson
Helen Riehl
Trudy Riffe
Bill Robertson
Mary Roche
Nancy Roedell
Sharon Romaneski
Charlotte Rosier
Nancy Rossman
Nancy Rossmeissl
Sandy Rowland
Ellen Roy
Nancy Meyer Sabari
Eleanore Sackmann
Sandra Saffran
Bobbie Sahr
Dianne St. Mary
Linda Salsbury
Wendy Samson
Mutt Scaman
Cathy Schmid
Barbara Schultz
Jenifer Fitterer Schultz
Judy Schussler
Charlene Scott
Barbara Sears
Eve Semon
Jean Sentz
Ileen Shields
Kimberly Shinn
Erin Shirey
Donna Shore
Cristi Silvas
Susan Simonson
Kristine Sims
Mary Skinner
Betty Smith
Kathleen Smith
Kathy Smith
Kirsten Smith
Sharon Smith
Vicki Smith
Jackie Snyder
Jenny Snyder
Nadine Snyder
Kathy Souder
Joan Sousley
Theo Mays Sowter
Mary Vee Splawn
B. J. Sprague
Karen Stebbins
Janni Stelzer
Sally Stephens
Lynda White Stepniewski
Lorrie Stetson
Beda Stewart
Jan Stohr
Cindy Strait
Mary Strausz
Norma Styner
Marcia Suko
Alice Summers
Sue Sutton
Midge Swainson
Marcia Swedin
Betty Taylor
Janet Tjarnberg
Julie Toney
Katherine Tuesley
Jean Tunstall
Barbara Underwood
Jean Vanek
Mary Ann Vanwert
Karin Van Wormer
Jackie Velikanje
Mary Velikanje
Lenore Vincent
Anita Volker
Lucetta Walker
Julie Ward
Dorothy Warren
Gail Weaver
Mary Jean Weigand
Mary Weyrick
Helen Whiting
Betty Wight
Pam Wilcox
Julie Williams
Mary Williams
Anne Marie Willis
Suzie Winn
Dorothy Wolf
Susie Woodin
Carol Woolf
Mary Wright
Harriet Yandt
Becky Yeaman
Harriet Young
Margaret Zimmerman
Pat Zirkle
Debbie Zulauf

N·O·R·T·H·W·E·S·T F·R·E·S·H

Junior League of Yakima, Inc., 5000 West Lincoln, Yakima, Washington 98908

Name ____

Address ____

City ______________________ State ________ Zip ____________

Please send me __________ copies of NORTHWEST FRESH
at $13.95 per copy . . . . ____________

Washington Residents add 7.5% sales tax at $1.05 per copy . . . . ____________

Shipping and handling at $2.25 per copy . . . . ____________

TOTAL ENCLOSED ____________

Please make check payable to NORTHWEST FRESH, and send to above address.

Proceeds from the sale of NORTHWEST FRESH will benefit programs sponsored by the Junior League of Yakima, Inc.

N·O·R·T·H·W·E·S·T F·R·E·S·H

Junior League of Yakima, Inc., 5000 West Lincoln, Yakima, Washington 98908

Name ____

Address ____

City ______________________ State ________ Zip ____________

Please send me __________ copies of NORTHWEST FRESH
at $13.95 per copy . . . . ____________

Washington Residents add 7.5% sales tax at $1.05 per copy . . . . ____________

Shipping and handling at $2.25 per copy . . . . ____________

TOTAL ENCLOSED ____________

Please make check payable to NORTHWEST FRESH, and send to above address.

Proceeds from the sale of NORTHWEST FRESH will benefit programs sponsored by the Junior League of Yakima, Inc.

N·O·R·T·H·W·E·S·T F·R·E·S·H

Junior League of Yakima, Inc., 5000 West Lincoln, Yakima, Washington 98908

Name ____

Address ____

City ______________________ State ________ Zip ____________

Please send me __________ copies of NORTHWEST FRESH
at $13.95 per copy . . . . ____________

Washington Residents add 7.5% sales tax at $1.05 per copy . . . . ____________

Shipping and handling at $2.25 per copy . . . . ____________

TOTAL ENCLOSED ____________

Please make check payable to NORTHWEST FRESH, and send to above address.

Proceeds from the sale of NORTHWEST FRESH will benefit programs sponsored by the Junior League of Yakima, Inc.